SKINNYCOOKS
CAN'T *Be* TRUSTED

SKINNYCOOKS CAN'T *Be* TRUSTED

Mo'Nique

with **Sherri McGee McCovey**

Recipe Consultant G. Garvin

AMISTAD *An Imprint of* HarperCollins*Publishers*

FIRST EDITION

Designed by Laura Klynstra
Food styling by Morgan Welebir
Food photography by Steven Moeder
Mo'Nique photography by Dan Chavkin
Mo'Nique wedding photography by Kevin McIntyre
Clothing worn on jacket by Linda Stokes
Snapshots courtesy of Mo'Nique

Library of Congress Cataloging-in-Publication Data
Mo'Nique.
Skinny cooks can't be trusted/by Mo'Nique & Sherri McGee McCovey; recipe consultant G. Garvin.
New York: Amistad, 2006.
p. cm.
ISBN-13: 0-978-0-06-112105-0
ISBN-10: 0-06-112105-3
1. Cookery, American. 2. Menus.

TX715 .M81165 2006
642′.4—22

2006044038

06 07 08 09 10 ❖/CCW 10 9 8 7 6 5 4 3 2 1

This book is dedicated to all those who aren't afraid to eat.

Mo'Nique

CONTENTS

ACKNOWLEDGMENTS

Mommy, thanks for years of pots filled with love. Daddy, thanks for letting Mommy experiment on you so she could get it right for us.

Mimmie, you could take a hot dog and make it delicious.

Shalon, thanks for eating Mommy's food even when you knew it wasn't good. David and Jonathan, you haven't experienced Mommy's cooking yet, but you're both in for a treat. I've gotten better since your big brother.

Sid, what can I say, you've been my rock for twenty-five years. Thank you.

Steve, stop trippin', we all know Kelly is the real cook in your family… so your Steve Steak Imes should really be Kelly's.

Miss Cori and Veronica, I couldn't do any of this without the two of you. Thank you for your support and for loving me and my babies so much!

Rhonda, the early morning breakfasts have always been truly appreciated and right on time. But after 9 A.M., it's Rita's kitchen.

Miss Rita, you truly missed your calling. You should've been a chef… or a bartender… or a pole dancer. I'll just leave it at that. Thanks for so many wonderful meals.

Dee Dee, your hands are made of magic and my face always looks magical. Thank you.

Patrice, I don't know how you do it, but you work the hell out of my hectic schedule. I appreciate you.

Allen "Bam" Holley, brother, keep watchin' those karate flicks while enjoying one of our recipes. You'll get to use them one day.

Terrell, my "Smiley," I'm proud to know you. Keep growing!

Michelle and Yolonda, we're all big girls. Thanks for sharing my life, love, and food.

Sherri McGee McCovey, once again you've taken my life and made magic, even when I may have made it extremely difficult. Now I understand all the questions and the method to your brilliant madness. Thanks for making me answer them and for always having my back.

G. Garvin, thanks for making it good all the time.

Manie B., you said you'd take us to the *New York Times* bestsellers list and you've never let us down! Here we go again, brother!

Dawn Davis, Laura Klynstra, and Morgan Welebir at HarperCollins, it's been a pleasure to work with you. Until we meet again.

Thank you, Lord, for blessing me to live my dreams—working with great people—everyday!

To my wonderfully supportive mother, Mary A. McGee, thank you for always having a hot dinner on the table (even after a long workday) as I was growing up—and sometimes now, too. This one is for you.

To my father, the late John W. McGee. Daddy, I know you're smiling on me and I feel your presence daily! Thanks for being a fine example of a good man and a wonderful father. I miss you!

To the wonderful chefs in my family: grandmother Doris Smith, who can whip up a pie crust from scratch (and so many other things) in no time flat; my aunts Ruth and Donna, who, like true Southern belles always have tables full of good food; my aunts Ollie and Billie—the gumbo queens—I'm still waiting. Love to my uncles—Ellis, Quenion, Lee, and George—who always seem to show up the moment dinner is on the table. Mother-in-law, Francene, your macaroni and cheese is hard to beat; and Aunt Betty McCovey, thanks for a few new culinary gems.

Mo'Nique, girl, we've done it once again! I'm so thankful that God put you in my life. Together we've done great things. I appreciate your loyalty, constant fight, sisterly love and support, continued encouragement, and damn good cooking. I've eaten too well and way too much. It's official. I'm on the team! But not for long!

Sara Finney-Johnson, you began as my mentor and boss and have grown into a treasured friend. Thanks for your support, prayers, and for teaching me the true meaning of a Proverbs 31 woman in the twenty-first century! I look forward to the future.

Shout-outs to my circle of good girlfriends: Camille Tucker, Stacey Evans Morgan, Chrystal Evans Bowman, Wendy Turner Codwell, Tiffany Avery Smith, Tamara "Buffy" Landry, Dominique Jennings, Kimberly Greene-Williams, Maria Guerrero-Freeman, Kim Adams, Diann Valentine, Kimberly Stephens (the black Emily Post), and Cheryl Chisholm. Okay, ladies, now we have no excuse not to cook for our mates (and the ones on the way)!

To my boy Gerry "G." Garvin, a true Hollywood chef, thanks for some wonderfully delicious meals over the years at your fine establishments, and for always keepin' it real (except for the carrots and wine in the collard green recipe). You're a truly talented brother! Mama and 'em taught you well!

Steve Imes, thanks for the offer back in 2001 to write our first book. You've changed my life in so many ways and I am eternally grateful. Kelly, big ups to you, too, for sharing so many of your culinary secrets. The oxtails look delicious.

Mr. and Mrs. Imes, it was truly a joy to work with you and share in your wonderful family stories and recipes.

Dawn Davis, Laura Klynstra, and Morgan Welebir at HarperCollins, thanks for jumping right in and helping to make this project fly. You outdid yourselves.

To the best damn agent in the publishing game, Manie Barron (a.k.a. Manie B.) of the Menza Barron Literary Agency, you've had our backs from day one! We'll always have yours, too!

And last, but certainly not least, to the love of my life, my handsome husband, Anthony McCovey. Honey, thanks for your patience, love, support, and for always graciously sampling whatever's cooking on the stove! I got it right this time, baby! And I also got it on the cover! Love you!

Sherri McGee McCovey

INTRODUCTION

When it comes to good food, I've never been one of those finicky eaters who has to know how many calories are in a dish before I sit down and enjoy. In fact, it really doesn't matter if it's made from scratch or comes out of a can with the words "Chef Boyardee" on the label. As long as it smells good, looks good, and tastes good, it's all good with me.

I grew up on crispy fried chicken, pigs' tails and sauerkraut, corn pudding, crab legs, and oyster stew. Back in the day, that's what dinnertime was about—food that filled you up. Well, welcome back to the good old days with a cookbook that celebrates rich, hearty family favorites (and a few that have become favorites) made with all the butter, eggs, cream, flour, sugar, ham, whipped cream, ice cream, chocolate chips, and cows (yes, you read right, cows) that give food those delicious flavors. You know, like taste, which, over the years, has been eliminated from a lot of food, thanks to killjoys like the no-carb diet, the low-fat diet, the no-sugar plan, and the low-salt diet. Hell, that's no fun. Neither are folks who skimp on the shrimp, bypass the bacon, and forget to sample the soup when they're whipping up a meal. Baby, I don't trust any cook who isn't at least 200 pounds—and you shouldn't either.

That's why I've written *Skinny Cooks Can't Be Trusted*, a cookbook for those like me who desire food with flavor, like chocolate and cream, sugar and butter, and everything in between, rather than slimming substitutes that seldom satisfy, like two percent milk instead of heavy cream, cottage cheese rather than rich ricotta, and margarine in place of good, old-fashioned butter. In *Skinny Cooks Can't Be Trusted*, if the recipe calls for a stick of butter, then, believe me, that's what's going in—the whole stick. I'm talking about finger-lickin'-good fare that'll have folks scrapin' the pots for fourths and fifths (seconds and thirds are a given for some big girls—if we pace ourselves). Take it from me, a fabulous feast can turn a bad day into a damn good one, especially if it's made with TLC (that's tender loin chops), or tomatoes, lettuce, and cheese. Yes, these recipes are rich, which means that unless you get your workout on (like I do regularly), they're not meant to be eaten every day!

And unlike some cookbooks that simply list ingredients, this is the ultimate kitchen companion, offering everything from soups to sweets, fond—and funny—food memories, time-saving cooking tips, and favorite food shortcuts (because, let's face it, no one has time to cook *everything* from scratch, but that doesn't mean it shouldn't taste like you did) for those who may be cu-li-nar-i-ly challenged.

And because I'm your girl, it's all arranged into complete menus ideal for every occasion (and perfected by my good friend and chef G. Garvin of TV One's popular cooking show *Turn Up the Heat)*. Use the Man Catcher if your mission is to get married, the Morning-After Breakfast if the lovin' was so damn good it inspired you to get up and cook, or the *Other Morning-After Breakfast* if you were far from inspired—more like insulted. *Skinny Cooks Can't Be Trusted* also features dinner parties, a classic Sunday Supper, a romantic Valentine's Day soiree, and much more.

I've already told you that skinny women are evil. Now I'm letting you know that they can't be trusted—especially in the kitchen. It's time to break out the blenders, grab the mixing bowls and spatulas, and get ready for some laughs and down-home cooking as only a BIG girl who loves to eat can bring it to you, baby—with *no damn substitutes*.

Bon appétit,

Mo'Nique

The
MAN CATCHER

If you cook for a man, he'll be yours for life—especially if you throw down the way his mama does. So the question isn't whether you *should* cook, it's what the hell to prepare that makes all the difference in the world. Take it from me, that adage "the way to a man's heart is through his stomach" is no damn joke—and neither is my Man Catcher menu. Baby, this one'll get you a wedding ring. Now how big a ring depends on how well you do it, so pay attention.

I discovered the merits of the Man Catcher while dating my second husband back in the early nineties. He was a regular at Mo'Nique's Comedy House, the club I eventually owned at 225 North Liberty Street in the heart of downtown Baltimore. Before it became a comedy hot spot, Mo'Nique's was a Persian restaurant. The owner was cool and he'd let us host comedy two nights a week. After a while, things went so well and we got so popular that the owner eventually sold us the place—debt and all. But we were happy to have it. And as with all of our endeavors, Mo'Nique's was a family-owned-and-operated enterprise. My brother, Steve (who worked as an analyst with the FBI by day), served as the club's manager along with our friend, Kenny "Big Papa" Young. The two of them did anything and everything to keep the doors open. My mother, whom we affectionately call Miss Alice, collected money at the door (and if necessary, baby, she served as security, too).

On the surface, Mo'Nique's was a beautiful place and on weekends, we were packed. But venture a little further behind the scenes into the kitchen and it was quite a different story. Though our chef, Dwight, did a wonderful job whipping up some of the most fabulous fare in town, there were pressing problems—a gaping hole in the middle of the kitchen floor, constant water leaks, and an ice machine that stayed on the blink (we quickly learned that warm bourbon made the jokes funnier). How we managed to stay open for three years without being cited for health code violations can only be attributed to Steve and Big Papa's creative management, I'm sure.

But I was proud of the fact that Mo'Nique's served the best food in town. Our signature dish, the Mo Burger, was probably the most popular dish on the menu, and I don't know too many comedy clubs that serve rice pilaf and crab balls (hey, this is Baltimore, you gotta have crab). The three years we were in business were some of the best of my career. Mo'Nique's was a place where up-and-coming comics like Steve Harvey and Michael Colyar would show up for five minutes in the spotlight. We had plenty of regulars and my second husband was one of them.

The first night he came in, he told my mother he was going to marry me one day. When I found out, I was flattered because, though short, he was a cutie. Marriage, however, was the last thing on my mind. I had already been down that road. But he eventually won me over and we began dating. When things really started to heat up, I thought it was only right to cook dinner for him. You know, to prove how well-rounded a woman I was (in more ways than one). Ladies, cooking for a man is serious business. And though I'd cooked for plenty of dates, this one was potential husband material, which meant I had to pull out all the stops.

I initially thought I'd serve short ribs, but ruled that out in case he had a Napoleonic complex. Rather than make a wrong move, I decided to consult my beloved grandmother on my daddy's side, Mimmie, who is a master chef in our family. Growing up, I had a ball playing in her beautiful clothes and eating her good food. People say that I take after her. Short, round, with a head full of white curls, Mimmie's got the most beautiful brown skin I've ever seen. She's also had her share of husbands, which meant, to me, that she knew how to cook. So I decided to call her and find out what I should prepare. With Mimmie, though, you get a thousand questions before she'll answer yours.

"Is he short or tall?"

"Short, but cute, Mimmie," I said, wondering what difference height made.

"How long you two children been dating?"

"A few months."

"You like him a lot?"

"Yes, ma'am," I said.

"You think he's *the one?*" Mimmie continued.

"Yes, ma'am," I replied, hoping she'd get to the answer soon.

"Well, there's really only one meal to make."

"What's that?" I asked, intrigued.

"You gotta make him the Man Catcher."

Turns out, the Man Catcher is a tried-and-true family tradition. Legend has it, Mimmie prepared it to land her first two husbands (before they passed on) and for Big Daddy, her third husband. Big Daddy and Mimmie were together thirty-five years until his death. When my parents were dating, Miss Alice made the menu for my father, and forty-two years later they're still going strong and she still cooks dinner every night. The story goes that my mother undercooked the chicken, and my father, not wanting to hurt her feelings, smothered it with hot sauce to make it edible. Now that's some real love right there.

With all of these success stories the Man Catcher sounded like a winner. So I got to it, frying up drumsticks, breasts, thighs, and wings, boiling macaroni, grating cheese, picking and cleaning collard greens, and mixing cornbread batter. Baby, after a couple of hours in that hot little kitchen, I was so damn tired I couldn't see straight. The thought of making a peach cobbler from scratch was out of the question. So I did the next best thing—I recruited Mimmie to make one of hers.

Now, if the thought of cooking an entire meal from scratch has you scratchin', then baby, don't be afraid to recruit some help. It doesn't matter whether it comes from your mama, grandmama, that special auntie that brings the good desserts to the family gatherings, or from the neighborhood bakery. All that matters is that it tastes good. But whatever you do, make sure to dispose of the evidence (outside, in the back, around the corner, burn it if you have to). Remember, your goal is to catch that man and the last thing you want is to get caught with a Mrs. Smith's frozen apple pie box in the trash can. The fact that you didn't cook the entire meal from scratch is not a crime. Getting caught is. (Now listen, before all the haters start saying that not makin' it from scratch is starting the relationship out on a lie, understand that I *did* know how to make a peach cobbler from scratch, but time and energy weren't on my side.)

After slavin' away in that hot little kitchen all I wanted to do was lie down and take a nap. But I resisted. And when my date arrived, I was refreshed and looking great (that's part of the

Man Catcher, you've gotta look good, too). I showed him in and when he got a whiff of all that good home cooking, his knees got weak. We sat down and when he saw that beautiful spread, baby, he smiled, grabbed a plate, loaded it up like he hadn't eaten in weeks, and got to work. It felt good to see him enjoy himself so much and I enjoyed myself right along with him. After a second—and a third—helping, we moved to the living room and got more comfortable before I pulled Mimmie's pipin' hot peach cobbler from the oven and topped it with a side of Häagen-Dazs vanilla ice cream. With a full stomach, he laid back on the sofa and asked if he could kick off his shoes and get even more comfortable. I said, "Let me do that for you" and helped him. We talked, but he started to doze in midsentence. As tired as I was, I dozed right along with him. That's when I knew the Man Catcher was a winner.

I later found out that it was really Big Daddy's recipe and that Mimmie wasn't really the chef—Big Daddy was. She just changed it from the Woman Catcher to the Man Catcher. Either way, it didn't take long for my man to propose after that. Before I knew it, I was making home-cooked meals regularly and he was enjoying them. But my career began to heat up. Spending hours in the kitchen was the last thing on my agenda—and so was marriage. Though it didn't work out for us, I still swear by the merits of the Man Catcher and the results. But be careful. It's one of those menus to pull out of the arsenal only when you're certain the man you're trying to catch is truly the one.

Without further ado, the Man Catcher!

Mo'Nique

Fried Chicken

10 pieces chicken

5 cups all-purpose flour

1 teaspoon salt

1 teaspoon seasoning salt

1 teaspoon freshly ground black pepper

1 teaspoon Old Bay seasoning

5 cups canola oil

Fried Chicken
Mouthwatering Macaroni and Cheese
Collard Greens with Smoked Turkey
Cornbread Muffins
Peach Cobbler
Serves 4

The day before, fill a container with ice and water and submerge all the chicken in the ice bath. Cover and place in the refrigerator.

When you are ready to prepare the chicken, remove the chicken from the ice bath and pat the pieces dry. In a deep bowl or paper bag, combine the flour and all of the seasonings. Set aside. Place the oil in a deep skillet or pot over high heat. Coat the chicken with the flour, shaking off the excess, and gently drop 4 to 5 pieces into the hot oil. (A good way to test if the oil is hot enough, is to drop a pinch of flour into it and see if it starts to sizzle.) Make sure to submerge the chicken completely. Cook for 15 to 18 minutes, turning the pieces occasionally. Remove the cooked chicken to some paper towels to absorb the excess oil.

⇥ MO'S OPTION ⇤

You can also finish the chicken off in the oven. Cook the chicken in the oil for only 6 to 7 minutes on each side. Remove to a baking sheet and bake in a 350-degree oven for about 4 minutes.

Mouthwatering Macaroni and Cheese

Salt

2 pounds elbow macaroni

Freshly ground black pepper

1 handful dried parsley flakes

1 jar Old English sharp cheese spread

1 jar (8 ounces) Cheez Whiz

About 1 pound sharp Cheddar, grated (4½ cups)

6 tablespoons butter (more doesn't hurt, but don't go overboard).

1 large egg

1 cup milk

Preheat the oven to 350 degrees.

Bring a large pot of salted water to a boil. Add the pasta and cook until just chewy (don't let it get too soft), about 8 minutes. Drain the pasta, season with salt and pepper and the parsley, and set aside. Grease a casserole dish with a little of the butter and spread half of the macaroni in the bottom of the dish. Top the macaroni with half of each of the cheeses, and 3 or 4 pats of butter. Repeat the procedure with the rest of the pasta and the remaining cheese and butter.

Whisk the egg and milk together and pour the mixture over the macaroni and cheese. Bake, uncovered, for 20 to 25 minutes, until bubbly and golden brown on top.

Mo'Nique

Collard Greens with Smoked Turkey

¼ cup olive oil

2 or 3 turkey tails

1 medium yellow onion, diced

3 garlic cloves, minced

2 shallots, minced

2 cups chicken stock

3 bunches collard greens

1 teaspoon salt

1 teaspoon freshly ground black pepper

1 teaspoon seasoning salt

3 hot sport peppers, or 1 teaspoon crushed red chili pepper, optional (but it adds a kick)

1 teaspoon sugar, optional

Heat the olive oil in a large stockpot over high heat. Add the turkey tails and sauté briefly. Add the onion, garlic, and shallots, and sauté another minute or two. Add the chicken stock and 1 cup of water and bring to a boil; reduce to a simmer over medium heat.

While the turkey tails are simmering, separate and wash the greens thoroughly. Remove the stems. Stack 6 to 8 leaves on top of each other and roll (as if rolling a cigar). Cut the rolled greens into pieces a little narrower than an inch.

Place the greens in the pot with the stock. Make sure the greens are covered completely—if not, add more stock. Season with salt, pepper, and seasoning salt. Add the hot peppers and sugar, if using. Simmer 30 minutes over medium heat, stirring occasionally to evenly distribute the meat. Taste to confirm that the greens have reached the desired tenderness.

⊰MO'S OPTIONS⊱

Though this recipe calls for collards, I like to mix in turnip greens as well. If you're from the South and can't do greens without vinegar, then top your finished greens off with a shake or two. You can find turkey tails at your local supermarket. If you don't see tails, turkey wings work well, too.

Cornbread Muffins

2 cups yellow cornmeal

½ cup all-purpose flour

2½ teaspoons baking powder

Pinch of salt

1 tablespoon sugar

¼ cup vegetable oil

1 large egg

1¼ cups whole milk

Preheat the oven to 350 degrees.

Mix the cornmeal, flour, baking powder, salt, and sugar in a large bowl. Add the oil, egg, and milk. Beat with a wooden spoon or a metal whisk for 30 to 40 seconds, until smooth. Grease a muffin pan and fill each cup with batter about two-thirds full. Bake until a toothpick poked in the center of one of the muffins comes out clean, 35 to 40 minutes. Remove from the oven and let cool for 15 minutes.

8

⊰MO'S OPTIONS⊱

If you're short on time, Jiffy corn muffin mix will do. Real corn kernels added to the batter make it taste even better. Stir ½ cup fresh or frozen corn kernels (thawed) into the batter before baking.

Mo'Nique

Peach Cobbler

FILLING

10 cups canned peaches (with juice)

1 cup sugar

1 teaspoon ground nutmeg

2 teaspoons ground cinnamon

2 tablespoons unsalted butter

2 teaspoons vanilla extract

Juice of 2 lemons

3 tablespoons all-purpose flour

COBBLER DOUGH

2 cups all-purpose flour, plus extra for kneading the dough

2 teaspoons baking powder

¼ teaspoon salt

½ cup solid vegetable shortening (like Crisco)

½ cup buttermilk

EGG WASH

1 egg yolk

2 tablespoons heavy cream

To make the filling, pour the peaches and juice into a large pot and heat over medium flame. Add the sugar, nutmeg, cinnamon, butter, and vanilla extract. Mix well and cook for 3 to 4 minutes. Stir in the lemon juice and flour, letting it cook over low heat for 8 to 10 minutes. Once this is done, remove the peach mixture from the heat and set aside.

Preheat the oven to 350 degrees.

To make the dough, combine the flour, baking powder, and salt (a big fork works great for this). Once this is mixed well, cut in the shortening. Stir in the buttermilk thoroughly. Sprinkle a handful of flour onto a clean work surface and roll out the dough, making sure it is not too thin.

Transfer the peach mixture to a baking dish or individual ramekins. If you're using a baking dish, cut the dough into long 1-inch-wide strips and arrange in a lattice pattern over the top of the fruit. If you're making individual cobblers, cut the dough into rounds to cover the filling.

To make the egg wash, whisk together the egg yolk and the cream. Brush the dough with the egg wash, then bake for 30 to 45 minutes, until the crust is golden brown.

9

⊱MO'S TIP⊰

If you've got time, make the peach cobbler and the
macaroni and cheese the day before.

⊱MO'S BEVERAGE⊰

Sweet iced tea goes real well with this menu.

Mo'Nique

The
MORNING-AFTER BREAKFAST

Have you ever had one of those perfect evenings? No kids. No company. It's just you and your mate. He's looking good. You're feeling good, and before you know it upstairs you go to get busy and everything is just on point. Don't you love it when that happens? I know I do! Tell me, how do you feel the next morning? Happy? Sure. Loved? Hopefully. Hungry? Absolutely. That's what a good romp will do: inspire you to get up and fix a nice hearty breakfast.

Big girls know about this all too well. If you don't believe me, then put on any CD by my girl, neo-soul singer Jill Scott. Baby, Miss Jill is a master at extolling the virtues of romance and food in song. On her multiplatinum debut CD, *Who Is Jill Scott?*, she has a tune that I just love called "Exclusively." It talks about how she was so inspired after a night of extra-good lovin' from her man that the next morning she jumped up and rushed to the store for orange juice, croissants, and some butter and strawberries to take back home to him. She continued the food and romance trend on her follow-up CD, *Beautifully Human: Words and Sounds Vol. 2*, with another hot jam called "Whatever." Once again she informs her fans that she was so moved by the tricks her lover pulled out of his sleeve that she couldn't wait to fix him some chicken wings and some fish and grits as a fitting reward for how he put it on her. Baby, like Jill, I can relate to that sentiment because, for me, a good breakfast always enhances the morning after a wonderful night.

From the moment I heard Jill's melodic voice on her debut CD, I became a fan. And I was especially thrilled when my favorite magazine, *Essence*, arranged for us to sit down together to talk for one of their cover stories. We talked for hours and I fell in love with that sistah even more because in addition to being cool, I felt like it was the beginning of a wonderful friendship, which is why I was especially touched when she penned a special poem for this book.

Thanks, Jilly from Philly! Love you, sis!

P. Pie

I got something for you honey
I made it by myself
I don't know the nutritional value
But I know it's good for your health
This is a very special dish
Only your lips can taste
Take your time and enjoy my love
Let nothing go to waste
It's as sweet as a ripe nectarine
Sometimes fuzzy like a peach
It's as juicy as a watermelon
But it hasn't got any seeds
It's as hot as midsummer's noon
More wet than morning dew
It's spread out all decorative
And it's waiting just for you.

—*Jill Scott*

Mo'Nique

Blueberry Pancakes

5 cups all-purpose flour

¼ cup sugar

1½ tablespoons baking powder

1½ teaspoons salt

5 cups whole milk

4 large eggs

5 tablespoons unsalted butter, melted

1 pint blueberries

Maple syrup (see Mo's Tip)

Blueberry Pancakes
Fluffy Scrambled Eggs with Green Onions
Home Fries
Turkey bacon (store-bought)
Fresh-squeezed orange and cranberry juice
(see Mo's Beverage, page 15)
Serves 4

Whisk the flour, sugar, baking powder, and salt together in a large bowl. Gradually whisk the milk into the dry ingredients, followed by the eggs. Mix in 3 tablespoons of the melted butter and reserve the remaining 2 tablespoons.

Heat a griddle or two large, heavy nonstick skillets over medium heat. Brush lightly with the reserved butter. Working in batches, pour the batter by ¼ cupfuls onto the griddle. Sprinkle each pancake with a handful of blueberries. Cook until the bottom side turns brown, about 1½ minutes. Turn the pancakes and cook until the second side browns, about 1 minute. Accompany with maple syrup and plenty of butter.

⊰ MO'S OPTION ⊱

For a quick (and good) store-bought pancake batter,
Bisquick Shake 'n Pour blueberry pancake mix is the way to go!

⊰ MO'S TIP ⊱

I love to warm my syrup up in the microwave.

13

SKINNYCOOKSCAN'T *Be* TRUSTED

Fluffy Scrambled Eggs with Green Onions

6 large eggs

1 tablespoon heavy cream

1 tablespoon olive oil

Pinch of garlic salt

Pinch of salt

Freshly ground black pepper

1½ teaspoons butter

3 green onions, white part only, chopped

Crack the eggs into a medium bowl. Pour the cream into the eggs and whisk, breaking down the egg yolks. Heat a sauté pan over medium heat for about 45 seconds, then add the olive oil. Pour in the eggs, moving them around in the pan with a wooden spoon or heat-proof spatula so they form creamy curds. Season with the garlic salt, salt, and pepper. Cook the eggs for 3 to 4 minutes. To finish them, add the butter and the green onions, remove from the heat, stir briefly, and serve. For softer eggs, cook a little less.

Mo'Nique

Home Fries

4 Idaho potatoes (about 2 pounds)
1½ tablespoons olive oil
½ teaspoon minced garlic
2 tablespoons diced Vidalia onion
Salt and freshly ground black pepper

Peel the potatoes and cut into small cubes. Place in cold water and set aside.

Heat a skillet over high heat for about 1 minute. Add the olive oil, garlic, and onion, and sauté briefly. Drain the potatoes, then add them to the skillet. Season with salt and pepper. Cover the pan and sauté for 10 to 12 minutes, until the potatoes are browned and tender. Test the potatoes for doneness. Serve hot right from the pan.

►MO'S BEVERAGE◄

Squeeze oranges a day ahead and store the juice in the refrigerator. A medium orange will give about 1/3 cup of juice, so you will need about 12 oranges for 4 servings. Mix equal parts fresh-squeezed orange juice and cranberry juice and serve in chilled champagne glasses. Kick up the morning drink with a splash of champagne.

SKINNYCOOKSCAN'T *Be* TRUSTED

The
OTHER MORNING-AFTER BREAKFAST

Now, I don't want to give the impression that I'm a loose woman, but I've lived a life filled with exciting escapades. Some have put a smile on my face and a little pep in my step, but there have been others that have left me pissed and puzzled—like an encounter with a "five minute" man who had the nerve to roll over and ask, "Girl, what's for breakfast?" I wanted to shout, "Wheaties." But that's the breakfast of champions and he certainly wasn't one. Instead of really letting him know what I thought of his performance, I stumbled into the kitchen and put the same effort into preparing breakfast as this one had put into the evening—none. Baby, when he sat down at the table, expecting the Morning-After Breakfast, he got what he deserved—the *Other* Morning-After Breakfast, a bowl of lumpy oatmeal.

Listen, if you must be the bearer of bad news, don't worry about how to deliver it. Let the food get the job done. This menu speaks loud and clear. It also works beautifully on bad-ass kids, too. Enough said!

Lumpy Oatmeal

Serves 4

1½ cups rolled oats (Quaker Oats)

2 tablespoons unsalted butter

2 tablespoons sugar (skip it if you want to make a point)

1 tablespoon pure honey (none if he doesn't deserve it)

2 tablespoons heavy cream

Bring 4 cups of water to a boil in a medium pan. Whisk in the oatmeal. Once the oatmeal is thoroughly mixed, adjust the heat to a simmer and cook for 20 minutes. Add the butter, sugar, honey, and cream (if he deserves it), mix well, and simmer for 10 to 12 minutes more.

⨕MO'S OPTIONS⨕

Okay, maybe he (or she) isn't a bad lover all the time. It was just an off night. Hey, it happens to the best of us. If a warning is the way to go, here are a few appetizing additions that show you still care: caramelized walnuts, toasted pecans, sliced bananas, or chocolate chips.

Romantic
RENDEZVOUS FOR TWO

There's a song by Teena Marie, "I'm a Sucker for Your Love," that describes me to a tee. There's no better feeling than lovin' someone and gettin' good lovin' in return (I stole that line from another prolific vocalist, Mr. Teddy Pendergrass). It may sound corny, but Teddy and Teena have the right idea. Holding hands, smoochin' under the stars, and cuddling up in bed with the love of my life while watching a movie (like my all-time favorite,

Claudine, starring the incomparable Diahann Carroll and the dashing James Earl Jones) is my idea of an intimate, cozy evening. And when I'm in love (and inspired), the lengths I'll go to show my affection are endless, but one thing's for sure—food is a consistent part of the amorous equation.

One of my most memorable trysts was a date with the man who is now my husband, Sidney. I've always been one of those people who have enjoyed coming home to a house full of folks. After all, that's what homes are all about: family and friends. Over the years, I've housed a struggling tap dancer chasing a dream, extended family tired of Baltimore winters, and even a singing group from the Bahamas trying to break into the business. (If you're reading this and thinking about contacting me, don't—those days are over and I've got enough folks to feed.)

This particular time, though, I wanted to spend a nice quiet evening alone with Sidney. Unfortunately, with so many people living in my house, that wasn't going to happen. So, instead of telling them all to get out, I left my own house. With an overnight bag in hand, I headed someplace where no one would find me: the ultraexclusive Hotel Bel-Air. The Bel-Air is one of the prettiest and most secluded hotels in Los Angeles, where I now live. I'm telling you, it's so tucked away that if you don't know where you're going, you will drive right past it. I love it because it's *the* perfect spot to just shut it down and chill. The grounds are lush, the service is impeccable, and the suites feature fabulous fireplaces perfect for getting a romantic party started. But all this luxury isn't cheap. You're gonna pay a pretty penny for the peace and privacy. This particular time, I didn't mind.

Ladies, the beauty of a romantic picnic is that it doesn't have to go down at the park, or on a beach (though they're wonderful places and I've done them all). It can take place in a luxury hotel suite or at a Best Western off the side of the freeway, if that's what's in your budget. The only rule when planning the perfect retreat is creativity. Back in the day, I got busy on top of the washing machine, with tennis shoes in it on the spin cycle (yes, for real)!

After settling into my room at the Bel-Air, I poured a glass of champagne, threw Tweet's *Southern Hummingbird* in the CD player, got comfortable in a plush terry robe, and then called room service to have a few tasty treats delivered. All that was needed was Sidney to make the evening complete. And when he arrived, looking fine as hell, it was. And it wasn't any of that wham-bam-thank-you-ma'am stuff. We got comfortable on a blanket that I spread out on the floor, and we talked, ate, drank, laughed, and enjoyed the evening—just the two of us. How did the evening go, you ask? A year later, our twins, David and Jonathan, arrived. So I'd say things went quite well.

When planning a romantic picnic, try a few of these feed-each-other foods. They'll set your romantic rendezvous in motion.

Mo'Nique

Deviled Eggs

10 large eggs

½ cup mayonnaise (see Mo's Tip)

3 tablespoons Dijon mustard

2 tablespoons sweet pickle relish

Pinch of paprika

**Deviled Eggs
Lobster Salad
Garlic Shrimp
Serves 2**

Bring a large pot of water to a boil. Gently add the eggs and cook for 12 to 15 minutes over medium heat. Remove the eggs from the water and cool. Peel the eggs and cut them in half lengthwise. Remove the cooked yolks to a small bowl and place the egg whites on a serving plate. Crush the yolks with a fork and stir in the mayonnaise, mustard, and relish. Scoop a spoonful of the yolk mixture into each egg-white half. Sprinkle with paprika and serve.

21

⊰ MO'S TIP ⊱

Add the mayonnaise by the tablespoon, not all at once,
to get the texture that you desire.

SKINNYCOOKSCAN'T*Be*TRUSTED

Lobster Salad

2 cups white wine

1 bay leaf

2 carrots, roughly chopped

3 stalks celery, roughly chopped

1 large onion, roughly chopped

1 (2-pound) live Maine lobster

1 head butter lettuce

1 head romaine lettuce

1 Hass avocado, chopped

2 ounces goat cheese, crumbled

1 orange, peeled and cut into segments

2 tablespoons toasted walnuts

1 tablespoon minced garlic, plus 4 cloves, crushed

3 basil leaves, finely chopped

Juice of 3 lemons

Pinch cayenne pepper

1 cup olive oil

Kosher salt

Crushed black peppercorns, about 1 teaspoon

Prepare a large bowl of ice and water. Fill a large pot with water and add the white wine, bay leaf, carrots, celery, and onions. Cover and bring to a boil. Plunge the live lobster into the water and cook for 12 to 15 minutes. Remove the lobster from the pot with tongs and submerge in the ice bath until cool. Remove the lobster meat from the shell and set aside.

Wash the lettuces and pat dry with paper towels. Cut the lettuce into bite-size pieces and place in a glass bowl along with the avocado, goat cheese, orange, and walnuts.

In a separate bowl, whisk together the minced garlic, basil, lemon juice, cayenne pepper, and ½ cup olive oil, seasoning to taste with salt and pepper.

In a small bowl, coat the lobster with the other ½ cup of olive oil, the crushed garlic, and salt and pepper, and place on a hot grill or grill pan for 3 minutes. While the lobster is grilling, pour half of the vinaigrette over the lettuce, toss, and spoon onto a large oval serving plate. Arrange the lobster around the salad and drizzle more vinaigrette over the top.

⊁ MO'S OPTION ⊱

If you're not down for cooking a live lobster, your local supermarket's seafood counter will probably carry cooked lobster.

Mo'Nique

Garlic Shrimp

1½ teaspoons olive oil

10 medium shrimp, peeled and deveined

1½ teaspoons minced garlic

½ cup white wine

2 tablespoons unsalted butter

Handful of chopped flat-leaf parsley

1 teaspoon diced shallots

Salt and freshly ground black pepper

Heat a sauté pan for 2 minutes. Add the olive oil to the pan and wait 5 seconds. Add the cleaned shrimp. Sauté over high heat for 30 seconds, then add the garlic. Sauté until the garlic is just browned. Pour in the white wine while moving the shrimp around in the pan. As the wine reduces, remove the shrimp to a small bowl and set aside while you finish the sauce. Add the butter, parsley, shallots, and salt and pepper to taste. Reduce the heat to low and simmer for 2 minutes. Put the shrimp back in the pan on medium heat to finish cooking for another 4 minutes. Serve in a small bowl.

23

⊁MO'S TIP⊱

There's lots of garlic here, so Altoids are a must.

⊁FOR A PERFECT PICNIC⊱

Champagne flutes, napkins, silverware, dishes (or none if it's a feed-each-other affair), candles, and your favorite *Slow Jams* CD help make for a special evening. People don't seem to take the time to get to know each other anymore. For a first date, a great conversation starter is the book *If . . . (Questions for the Game of Love)* by Evelyn McFarlane and James Saywell.

SKINNYCOOKSCAN'T*Be*TRUSTED

Steamed
CRAB BALTIMORE STYLE

Baltimore, Maryland, is the land of all things crab—from cakes, claws, and chowders, to legs, dips, and assorted soft-shell varieties—and my mouth waters just thinkin' about them all. As a crab connoisseur, I've noticed a distinct difference between crustaceans from the Chesapeake Bay and those from other parts of the country. Anyone who knows Maryland crabs knows they've got a sweet, hearty texture and are meatier than other kinds—and that's just the way food should be. They are widely considered the best-tasting crabs available, anywhere. To this day, I've never gotten enough, especially when there's a side of melted butter nearby.

Moving out west meant I wouldn't be able to get them whenever I wanted to, but I've found a few spots that'll do when I'm in need of a crab fix. One of my favorite restaurants, Crustacean, in Beverly Hills, California, offers a bowl of the tastiest Dungeness Crabs with Garlic Sauce and Secret Spices. I don't know what secret spices they add, but it's like an aphrodisiac every time I have it. If, however, I get a jones and only Maryland crab will do, then I'll pick up the phone and have a box delivered overnight.

My earliest recollection of falling in love with crab is of my father, who'd often pick them up for dinner from a spot back home called the Crab Shack on Monroe Street. Baby, the minute Daddy hit the door, we'd spread out the newspapers, pile the table high with those bright red crab legs, and eat until our hearts—and stomachs—were full. During long, hot Maryland summers, Daddy would steam them himself. And you couldn't tell him he wasn't *the* king of steamed crab. Most times, he'd get them just right and they'd be so juicy and tender we could suck the meat right out of the shells. But there were a few occasions when Daddy was off his game, and it was usually when he had a beer in his hand.

In the Southeast, folks take their steamed crab seriously, and to prepare crab just right, you need one key ingredient—beer. Not a fancy, expensive brew like Heineken or Guinness. We used the cheap, or shall I say inexpensive, brands like Miller Genuine Draft or Pabst Blue Ribbon. Now, while less expensive brews work beautifully on the crab, they have a far different effect on the folks doin' the steaming. My father, bless his heart, would get started early, popping open cans, and getting his sip on. And the more he drank, the more philosophical he became. In his mind, he'd be making profound statements but they didn't make a bit of sense to anyone else. The creators of *The Parkers* wrote him into a couple of episodes. He had a few cameos as a distinguished professor at Santa Monica College who sputtered on and loved to hear himself talk. I still chuckle at the thought of my father acting, especially since it wasn't much of a stretch. When friends would drop by, we'd just listen and laugh as they made the mistake of asking my father a simple question, not knowing they'd just opened a can of worms. Once, he asked a friend of mine, "What is good hair?" Luckily, she was smart enough to tell him what her grandfather taught her. "All hair is good hair as long as you got some." That was precisely the answer my father wanted to hear because this notion among black folks that straight hair is good hair drives my bald father crazy.

And crazy is exactly what it was in the kitchen when the time came for him to get started steaming crabs. After a six-pack, you couldn't tell him that perhaps he was in no shape to get the job done.

"Baby girl," he told me, "I was steaming crabs before you were born." All right then, playa. Handle your business.

With that said, he waltzed off to the kitchen. Now, the fact that more beer was going into my sweet father than into the pot was a summer tradition. One time, though, it was also a comedy of errors. The water was boiling, and Daddy was pouring in the beer—along with a little more for himself, too. But when he got ready to take those aggressive little crabs out of the box, it was as if they'd gotten together and decided they weren't goin' down without a fight. Baby, he went for one, and before he could get it in the water, another one flipped out of the box and onto the floor trying to get away. Stunned, he dropped the one he was holding. Before long, they had Daddy jumpin' around the kitchen, sidestepping them—and for a minute, the crabs were winning. This went on so long Daddy finally said, "Forget it," and sat down and opened another beer. When we came into the kitchen and witnessed this scene, all we could do was laugh and help finish the job.

Years later, when my brother Stevie and I moved west, we missed Baltimore crabs so much that we'd have them flown in, throw on some classic house music, and invite friends over for a West Coast version of our beloved summer tradition.

I'll never forget the first time my girlfriend and coauthor, Sherri McGee McCovey, came to one of our backyard parties. Now, Sherri's a cool sistah, but she's a city girl (and a graduate of Beverly Hills High, need I say more?). When I pointed her to the table, the first thing she said was, "Where're the plates?" I told her, "Girl, the table is your plate, so sit down and get busy." In no time, girlfriend was crackin' crabs like she was from B'More. The way we do it back home is that folks sit down, eat a while, get up and go about their business, and then come back for more whenever they want it. Crabbin' is an all-day activity and some of the best summertime eating there is.

Try your own version of our Steamed Crab Baltimore Style. There's nothing tricky about this one. Here, the crab is the star of the show. With a little Old Bay seasoning, the right beer, and a crab cracker (that's a utensil, not a food, y'all) you'll have a delicious dish in no time flat.

27

Steamed Crab

4 cups of your favorite beer

5 lemons, halved

1 tablespoon garlic salt

1 tablespoon kosher salt

4 to 5 pounds live blue crabs (16 to 20 crabs) (see Mo's Tip)

½ pound (2 sticks) butter, melted

Steamed Crab
Spicy Mayo
Cajun Rémoulade
Red Rooster Mayo
Serves 4

Bring 2 gallons of water to a boil in a large pot over high heat. Add the beer, squeeze and drop in the lemon halves, and season with the garlic and kosher salts. Drop the crabs into the water, cover, and return to a gentle boil. Cook for 9 to 12 minutes, until done. Remove the crab to a large serving platter and serve with the butter for dipping.

⇻ MO'S OPTIONS ⇺

For a tasty addition, crush 3 garlic cloves and add them to the melted butter, or try one of the following dipping sauces that I just love!

⇻ MO'S TIP ⇺

Ocean Pride Seafood in Lutherville, Maryland (www.oceanprideseafood.com), will ship blue crabs from the Chesapeake Bay to your door overnight.

28

Mo'Nique

Spicy Mayo

4 eggs (see Mo's Tip)

1 tablespoon white vinegar

1 tablespoon dry mustard

1 teaspoon salt

Juice of 1 lemon

1 cup canola oil

1 teaspoon minced garlic

Pinch of cayenne (if you like it spicy like I do, add more)

Separate the eggs, and put the yolks into a blender. (Reserve the egg whites for another use.) Blend the yolks until they are smooth. Add the vinegar, mustard, salt, and lemon juice, and mix together on low. Slowly add the oil, blending constantly. Make sure it doesn't break down and is nice and smooth. Eyeball it and use the oil accordingly. The more oil, the thicker the mayo. Add the minced garlic and cayenne and blend once more.

⇥ MO'S TIP ⇤

Some people (pregnant women, the elderly, the young, and people with impaired immune systems) should avoid foods made with raw eggs. Always keep mayonnaise refrigerated.

Cajun Rémoulade

1 cup store-bought mayonnaise

1 cup sour cream

1 teaspoon freshly ground black pepper

¼ cup diced white onions

3 tablespoons diced capers

Juice of ½ lemon

1 teaspoon sugar

2 tablespoons blacking spice

Mix together the mayonnaise and sour cream. Add the pepper, onions, capers, lemon juice, sugar, and blacking spice. Mix well and serve cold.

Mo'Nique

Red Rooster Mayo

4 eggs

1 tablespoon white vinegar

1 tablespoon dry mustard

1 teaspoon salt

Juice of 1 lemon

1 cup canola oil

1 teaspoon minced garlic

Pinch of cayenne (if you like it spicy like I do, add more)

Red Rooster hot sauce

Separate the eggs, and put the yolks into a blender. (Reserve the egg whites for another use.) Blend the yolks until they are smooth. Add the vinegar, mustard, salt, and lemon juice, and mix together on low. Slowly add the oil, blending constantly. Make sure it doesn't break down and is nice and smooth. Eyeball it and use the oil accordingly. The more oil, the thicker the mayo. Add the garlic, cayenne, and Red Rooster hot sauce to taste.

⤚MO'S BEVERAGE⤙

You can't do summertime crab without your favorite beer—
plenty of it, in a big ice chest.

The
"I'VE NEVER BEEN GOOD AT SAYING I'M SORRY" MEAL

There've been times when I've said things I regret. You know, Mouth Almighty, Tongue Everlasting. And when I get goin', I've got to say my piece and worry about the consequences later. Oftentimes, my instincts are right, but every now and then, I'm dead wrong. And although saying "sorry" has gotten easier over the years, sometimes it's easier to offer a palatable peace offering, instead.

The palatable peace offering is something Miss Alice (my mom) pulled on me while I was in the hospital awaiting the birth of the twins. One of them threatened to make his debut earlier than planned, and so it was to the hospital for me. Though I was flat on my back, my doctor told me I could eat whatever I wanted. That was all I had to hear. I lined up folks to bring lunch and dinner every day because that hospital food wasn't doin' it. I had my heart set, one Sunday, on Miss Alice's Tomatoes Stuffed with Crab and Shrimp. I asked my mother if she would mind fixing it for my Sunday dinner. That was on a Friday. By Sunday, baby, Miss Alice was tired (probably because she'd just returned from one of her frequent Vegas trips and didn't feel like cooking). Now, instead of telling me she wasn't up to it, she called the hospital room and did a sick bit that should've won her an Emmy for Outstanding Lead Actress in a Comedy Series. Baby, her performance was brilliant. I knew she wasn't sick, but I let her slide.

A few weeks later, when I returned home, don't you know the first meal she surprised me with was her stuffed tomatoes. I've never told my mother that I'm on to her fake coughs. Instead, I just accept—and enjoy—her palatable peace offerings.

This one is served cold on a bed of lettuce with boiled eggs and pickles. Delicious!

33

Tomatoes Stuffed with Crab and Shrimp

Serves 6

6 well-shaped medium tomatoes

Salt and freshly ground black pepper

1 pound small cooked shrimps

1 pound lump crabmeat, picked over for shells and cartilage

4 tablespoons mayonnaise

2 tablespoons Dijon mustard

1 teaspoon dry mustard

2 celery stalks, diced

4 teaspoons hot sauce, preferably Red Rooster

2 teaspoons Worcestershire sauce

Green onions, chopped (add your desired amount)

1 carrot, grated

2 tablespoons chopped flat-leaf parsley

Paprika

1 head lettuce

Green or black olives

6 hard-boiled eggs, shelled and quartered lengthwise

Pickles

Core the tomatoes: Remove the stem from each and slice a layer off the top to reveal the inside. Cut through the ribs of the tomatoes and remove the pulp, ribs, and seeds. Season the tomato shells with salt and pepper.

Chop the shrimp and mix with the crabmeat in a bowl. Stir in the mayonnaise, Dijon mustard, dry mustard, celery, hot sauce, Worcestershire, green onions, carrots, and parsley. Season well with the salt and pepper.

Stuff the tomatoes with the crab and shrimp mixture and sprinkle paprika on top. Place on a bed of washed and dried lettuce leaves and garnish the plate with the olives, eggs, and pickles. Refrigerate until cold and serve with crackers.

Baby,
YOU GOTTA GO

All breakups aren't bad ones. Sometimes they're necessary, especially when you discover that the love of your life is really a drug-addicted ex-con.

That's the predicament I found myself in a few years ago. I met this fine man on one of my many trips home to Baltimore from Los Angeles, and before I knew it we were living together, traveling together, and making plans to spend the rest of our lives together with a lavish wedding planned for the spring.

Now, it's been said that people show you who they are immediately. Well, this one did, only I was too in love to see all of the red flags waving in front of me—like the fact that, he confided during our intimate talks, he'd been locked up for embezzlement (he explained it as a white-collar crime that executives get away with every day), drugs (he only dabbled back in the day), gun possession (he was supposedly framed), and identity theft (he didn't do it). Okay, I know you're probably saying, "Damn, Mo, couldn't you see that brother was bad news?" That's the crazy thing about love. When you're in it, you make excuses for people and their crazy behavior, and you reason that those things are a part of a person's past. And that's exactly what I did. He seemed like the perfect man.

As the relationship progressed, however, things just didn't seem right—like the fact that I was illegally harboring a fugitive who never should've stepped foot out of the state of Maryland, and the fact that he was still a fan of white powdered substances—and I'm not talking about sugar. As much as I hated to admit that I had messed up with this one, I knew it was time for him to go when he started to nod in midsentence. Not only was he a danger to me, but also to my child.

Now, as wild as this relationship was, there were a few good times, and even though I had to end things, I didn't want it to go badly, especially since he was unpredictable. I've always found that if you drop the bomb over a good meal and offer a plate for later, the blow is softened—think of it as breaking up doggie-bag style. Since he was a fan of white substances, I decided to hook up my Fettuccine with Shrimp in Alfredo Sauce. Baby, he dug right in—but this was one time I just watched. After a few bites, I got up the nerve to tell him that the relationship wasn't working for me, that he had to leave my home immediately, and that his bags, along with a to-go plate and a motel reservation, were by the door. He wasn't happy about the breakup, of course (or about the security I had standing by in case something crazy jumped off), but I knew it was for the best.

There's no easy way to say good-bye, especially when feelings are involved and someone's about to get hurt. Even though the wedding was a month away, I went ahead with the reception and turned it into a "celebration of life" party—I was surrounded by friends and family who helped me get through this rough patch.

It took a minute to get over this one, partly because he harassed the hell out of me for months. But I learned a lot from the experience. Ladies, that's the beauty of life and love. You learn. You grow. You go on. And eventually you figure out that sometimes, you've got to send folks away in the spirit of love in order to find a new one.

Mo'Nique

Fettuccine with Shrimp in Alfredo Sauce

Serves 4

3 tablespoons olive oil

Salt

1 pound fettuccine

12 medium shrimp, peeled and deveined

Minced garlic

1 teaspoon chopped shallots

½ pound (2 sticks) unsalted butter

1 cup white wine

2½ cups heavy cream

½ teaspoon fresh thyme

1 teaspoon chopped flat-leaf parsley

Pinch dried rosemary

Grated Parmesan cheese (about 4 ounces)

Freshly ground black pepper

Bring 4 quarts of water to a boil over high flame. Add 2 tablespoons of the olive oil to the water with a double pinch of salt. Drop the pasta gently into the water and separate with a large fork so the pasta doesn't stick together. Reduce heat to a steady boil and cook for 7 to 10 minutes. Test for doneness and pull from the pot with tongs; cool in an ice water bath. Keep the hot cooking water for reheating the pasta when the sauce is ready.

Heat the remaining 1 tablespoon olive oil in a large sauté pan over high flame. Sauté the shrimp for about 1 minute, and remove from the pan and set aside. Turn the flame down and add the garlic, shallots, and 1 tablespoon of the butter to the pan. Sauté for 30 seconds. Add the white wine and simmer for 2 minutes; stir in the cream. While the cream simmers on low heat, add the herbs, the remaining butter (cut into pieces so it will incorporate easily), and half of the cheese. Mix well and season with salt and pepper.

As the cream sauce thickens, reheat the pasta briefly (10 seconds) in the cooking water. Drain the pasta and add with the shrimp to the cream sauce. Mix well, add more cheese, and serve.

⇥MO'S OPTIONS⇤

If shrimp isn't your thing, then try this one with chicken, veggies, or
sun-dried tomatoes. The technique remains the same.

These KIDS ARE WORKIN' MY NERVES

Feeding boys will put you in the poorhouse. And the fact that I've got four scares me. My oldest, a stepson, is twenty and out on his own. The youngest are just starting on solid foods, so I've got time. (One of them, Jonathan, takes after his mother—baby, that little boy could go through some Similac, and he requires a special formula, which is more expensive.) Then, there's my sixteen-year-old, Shalon, who, I swear, is trying to eat me out of house and home—and my home is quite large.

At six foot three, my baby is just as tall and fine as he wants to be. But unlike other kids his age, who can't get enough of tacos and pizza, or chicken fingers and french fries, Shalon wants ribs, steak, lobster, and crab legs with drawn butter—daily. And he will request what he wants, with no shame in his game. If I don't check him, Shalon will walk into a restaurant, find surf and turf on the menu—at market price, mind you—and order it like he's got the money in his pocket to pay for it. I'm all for good food, and steak and lobster are quite delicious. But damn it, those who like it that much should find a way to finance it sometimes. Yet trying to explain that to my son does no good. Neither does telling him, when he's out with friends and they're picking up the tab, not to order the most expensive thing on the menu. Baby, Shalon'll test that rule every single time.

He tested it so well, in fact, that all I could do was laugh when I heard about the stunt he pulled on a girlfriend of mine who took him for dinner at Red Lobster and told him to order whatever he wanted. That was the first mistake (you don't tell kids to pick what they want, you tell 'em what they can have). When the waiter came to take the order, my son proudly said he'd have the rock lobster tail with the grilled center-cut New York strip and a Shirley Temple. Embarrassed as hell, my girlfriend whispered that she couldn't afford that and asked him to pick something else. Well, Mr. Shalon acted as if he couldn't find anything else on the menu to order. I guess the waiter took pity on them because he brought Shalon the steak and lobster—for free! That's my son for you. Only Shalon could walk into the Red Lobster broke and walk out Thanksgiving-full without spending a dime.

Now, his behavior is probably my fault. During the lean years, before I was a "queen of comedy," I was the queen of making-a-little-go-a-long way. Most nights, Oodles of Noodles or franks and beans was our dinner of choice—and not because we really liked it. But as life changed, and big, fat juicy steaks were no longer out of reach, I wanted my baby to enjoy good food. Just not as much—or as often—as he'd like to. Shalon eats well most days, but every now and then, I like to take him back to our humble years.

Ladies, if you're a tired mother, like I am most days, and a five-course meal is out of the question, this is an excellent quickie. It won't win you any Mother of the Year awards but it will get the job done and get you some peace of mind in no time.

Mo'Nique

Spaghetti Casserole

Serves 4

6 tablespoons olive oil, plus more for the pasta water

Salt

2 pounds spaghetti

1 large white onion, chopped

2 pounds ground beef

Freshly ground black pepper

Garlic salt

1 (26-ounce) jar marinara sauce

3 tablespoons unsalted butter

1 cup grated Cheddar cheese (about 4 ounces)

Preheat the oven to 325 degrees.

Bring 4 quarts of water to a boil in a large pot over high flame. Pour in a generous splash of olive oil and a pinch of salt. Add the spaghetti and cook for about 7 to 10 minutes, until al dente.

While the pasta is cooking, heat a large saucepan over a medium flame. Add the olive oil, then the onion and ground beef. Season with salt and pepper, and the garlic salt, and simmer for 6 to 8 minutes. Pour in the marinara sauce and heat, stirring so it doesn't stick anywhere, then stir in the butter.

Add the cooked pasta to the meat sauce along with half the cheese. Mix well and pour into an oven-safe casserole dish. Sprinkle with the remaining cheese and bake for about 15 minutes, until browned and bubbly. Remove and serve.

⚔ MO'S OPTION ⚔

If you don't have spaghetti, whatever pasta you have in the pantry is fine.

⚔ MO'S TIP ⚔

Back in the day, Van Camp's Beanee Weenee, baked beans with
hot dogs, was a family staple, and still is, when all I feel like doing is
opening a can and warming dinner up.

Mo'Nique

Fight
PARTY AT MO'S

Over the years, my house has become the spot for fight parties. I guess a big den, big-screen TV, and a big kitchen means let's do it at Mo's. And that's fine by me, especially since I love to entertain. Whether it's a den of ten or a backyard of a thousand (which is about how many people showed up after I hosted the 2004 BET Awards—and rocked Beyoncé's "Crazy in Love" dance routine).

That night was such a high that I invited the entire studio audience and those watching at home to the after-party in my backyard if they could find the house, and when I entered my backyard, it looked like everybody had. There was a sea of people, standing shoulder-to-shoulder, eating, drinking and having one good ole time. I loved it. But I knew we were in trouble when police helicopters started to circle, shining light down on the crowd, and officers showed up at the house and told us we had to shut it down (after letting us slide a few hours earlier). That's the way I love to do things—big! Just not that big, ever again.

But fight parties are a different story. Back in the day, when Mike Tyson used to knock the hell out of folks, sometimes in the first round, we'd plan fight parties at my house. The menu was always crucial. Sometimes it was hot wings and pizza, but there was one party when someone suggested chili. Now, at the time, that sounded like a great idea. Chili's good. It's filling. It's easy to make; just plug in the Crock-Pot and in a few hours, dinner's done. There's just one problem, however. Chili doesn't agree with everyone's system. If you know this about yourself, don't dive in at a party and subject folks to the inevitable funk that's to follow. Bring something your stomach can handle—and make sure there is enough for everyone. At this chili party, the fight was in full effect and, surprisingly, it lasted more than two rounds. Everybody was getting their grub on. But by about round five, instead of a den of ten, we were four strong and holding. The six bathrooms in the house, thankfully, were enough to accommodate folks. But I knew it was time for them to get out of my house when someone tapped me on the shoulder and asked for a plunger. Clearly, chili was the wrong move, because it moved some folks in ways that just weren't right in mixed company.

If you and chili don't get along, be considerate and grab a bottle of Beano (so there'll be no surprises later), or hook this one up sans the beans.

Mo'Nique

Beef and Jalapeño Chili

1½ cups dried pinto beans, picked over and rinsed

¼ cup olive oil

2 tablespoons unsalted butter

2 white onions, chopped

4 garlic cloves, crushed

2 green bell peppers, seeded and chopped

2 jalapeño peppers, seeded and diced

3 pounds ground beef

Salt and freshly ground black pepper

1 bay leaf

1 teaspoon cayenne

2 tablespoons chili powder

1 (28-ounce) can crushed tomatoes

2 cups chicken stock

2 tablespoons tomato paste

Beef and Jalapeño Chili
Cheesy Cornbread Squares
Serves 4

45

The night before cooking, cover the beans with cold water and soak overnight.

Heat the olive oil and the butter in a large pot over high flame. Sauté the onions, garlic, peppers, and beef for 4 to 5 minutes. Season the mixture with salt and pepper. Add the beans, bay leaf, cayenne, and chili powder. Stir in the crushed tomatoes, the stock, 1 cup water, and the tomato paste. Bring to a high boil, then lower the heat and simmer for 45 minutes, until the beans are tender. Season with more salt and pepper if needed. Remove the bay leaf before serving.

For a spicy kick, I like to add some jalapeño sausage. Remove the meat from the casing, crumble, and add it to the beef. Or, substitute sausage for the ground beef altogether (use approximately 3 pounds of sausage). To cut down on prep time, use canned beans instead, which don't need soaking overnight. Reduce cooking time accordingly. This dish works just as well without the beans, too, for those with weak stomachs.

Mo'Nique

Cheesy Cornbread Squares

2 cups yellow cornmeal

½ cup all-purpose flour

Pinch of salt

2½ teaspoons baking powder

1 tablespoon sugar

¼ cup vegetable oil

1 large egg

1¼ cup whole milk

½ cup grated mild Cheddar cheese (about 2 ounces)

Preheat the oven to 350 degrees.

In a large bowl, mix together the cornmeal, flour, salt, baking powder, and sugar. Add the oil, egg, and milk, and beat with a wooden spoon or a whisk for 30 to 40 seconds, until smooth.

Grease a square baking pan. Pour the batter in and bake for 35 to 40 minutes. Remove from the oven and cool in the pan for 15 minutes. Cut the bread into small squares and place the squares on a baking sheet. Sprinkle a little cheese on top of each. Put back into the oven and bake for 5 to 7 minutes more, until the cheese melts.

Happy
VALENTINE'S DAY TO ME

Ladies (and gentlemen), let's say you find yourself dateless on the most romantic day of the year. Or, that someone special is acting like a special fool. Hey, it happens to the best of us. If you find yourself in this predicament, as I did one year after a relationship gone wrong, no one has to know you're dateless—unless you tell—and why on earth would you do that when you can do all of the things that make the day special anyway? Though disappointed, I refused to allow this minor setback to dictate my happiness. Hell, if I could call off a wedding a month before it was scheduled and go ahead with the reception anyway, surely I could get through one dateless Valentine's Day, and that's exactly what I did. Instead of moping, I spent the day taking care of the most important person in my life—me!

After a wonderful breakfast of scrambled eggs, turkey bacon, fresh fruit, and a mimosa, baby I put on my sexiest lingerie and an outfit to match my mood for the day—flirty—and headed to a day spa for an afternoon of pampering. After a relaxing massage (performed by a handsome masseur), a facial, and a full-body scrub that left me feeling fabulous, and famished, lunch was next on the agenda—along with a little shopping for something special.

Upon my return home, what was waiting on the doorstep? Why, a big, gorgeous arrangement of red roses from my favorite florist, and a card that read, "Happy Valentine's Day, beautiful." So what if I'd sent them to myself? No truer sentiment had been spoken and it made me feel damn good. That's the point of this day, right?

That evening, the magic continued as Luther Vandross serenaded me, candles lit up the house, the table was set, and I prepared for a cozy dinner for one—a dinner that started with succulent lamb chops and ended with decadent chocolate-covered strawberries and champagne. Full from the day and the delicious dinner, I made my way upstairs with a champagne glass in hand to finish off the evening. After a relaxing bubble bath, I pulled the pretty new gown I'd purchased from Victoria's Secret that afternoon out of the box, got in the bed and got romantic—all by myself—with another special purchase made that day. With a smile on my face, I fell off to sleep in no time.

Now that might not sound like the ideal Valentine's Day, but it was a perfectly fine way to love myself and reward my worth. Would I do it again? You damn right, and if you find yourself dateless on Valentine's Day (or any other day), by all means, you should, too.

Lamb Chops

3 tablespoons salt

3 tablespoons seasoning salt

3 tablespoons freshly ground
  black pepper

8 to 10 lamb chops

3 tablespoons olive oil

Lamb Chops
Mashed Potatoes with Chives
Chocolate-covered strawberries (store-bought)
Serves 4

Preheat the oven to 300 degrees.

Mix the salts and the pepper together and season the lamb chops on both sides. Pat the seasoning into the chops, so it sticks to the meat. Heat a large sauté pan over medium-high flame and add the oil. Be sure the oil is hot and place the chops gently in it. Cook for 3 to 4 minutes on each side. Transfer the pan to the oven and cook for 6 to 8 minutes more for perfect, medium-well chops.

≫ MO'S TIP ≪

A seasoned rack of lamb makes an elegant
presentation for dinner parties.

Mo'Nique

THE MAN CATCHER, PAGE 1

THE MORNING-AFTER BREAKFAST, PAGE 11

STEAMED CRAB BALTIMORE STYLE, PAGE 25

HAPPY VALENTINE'S DAY TO ME, PAGE 48

THE PERFECT ONE-POT PLEASER, PAGE 57

HOME FOR THE HOLIDAYS, PAGE 69

CARD PARTY GET-DOWN, PAGE 95

PEACH COBBLER, PAGE 9

Mashed Potatoes with Chives

7 Idaho potatoes, about 3 pounds
Salt
1 cup heavy cream
1 stick unsalted butter
Freshly ground black pepper
¼ cup finely chopped fresh chives

Peel the potatoes and place them in cold water as you go, to prevent discoloring. Once all the potatoes are peeled, cut them into medium-size cubes, place in a large pot, and cover with cold salted water. Bring to a boil and cook for 15 to 20 minutes, until tender when pierced with a fork. Drain the potatoes thoroughly and mash. Stir in the cream and butter, mixing well. Season with salt and pepper and mix in the chives before serving.

⊁MO'S TIP⊱

If your aim is to make a baby, throw on Barry White's *Love Songs* and press Shuffle. If it's a first date, crooner KEM is a great choice.

⊁MO'S BEVERAGE⊱

A chilled glass of Asti Spumante.

⊁MO'S MANTRA⊱

"If it doesn't feel good, forget it."

The
PERFECT BIRTHDAY DINNER PARTY

When it comes to birthdays, I'm all about gettin' my party on. Perhaps that's because at age twenty-one, when I was finally able to legally go to a bar and drink, I was married and about to become a mother. There was no big party. No friends around to take me to the strip club and help me make it official. Nowadays, when December 11 rolls around, you can usually find me cuttin' loose and gettin' my party on!

The year I turned thirty-five, my son Shalon was living with his father, which meant that for the first time, I was footloose and fancy-free to do whatever my heart desired. So, it was off to the Bahamas, where I partied until the wee hours of every morning with drink in hand and a fine Bahamian man on my arm. I guess I'm still making up for lost time because the years just seem to fly by. Every year that I'm still here is reason enough to celebrate with those who are special. Whether it's a weekend on some sunny island where I can laze the days away on the beach with friends (or just one special friend), or a dinner party at my house where we break out the good glasses and china (which you should use every day, anyway), birthdays are special. So, celebrate. And whatever you do, make it memorable!

Grilled Asparagus

Salt

2 bunches asparagus, trimmed

1 teaspoon olive oil

Freshly ground black pepper

Grilled Asparagus
Grilled Salmon with Crab and Brie
Red Velvet Cake
Serves 4

Bring a large pot of water to a boil and add a generous pinch of salt. Leaving the rubber band on, drop the asparagus bunches into the water and cook for 6 minutes. Meanwhile, prepare an ice bath. Remove the asparagus from the pot and submerge in the ice bath to cool. Remove the rubber bands and drain well. Coat the asparagus with the oil, season with the salt and pepper, and grill on a stove-top grill pan for 3 minutes on each side.

53

Grilled Salmon with Crab and Brie

2 tablespoons olive oil

4 ounces lump crabmeat, picked over for
    shells and cartilage

1 teaspoon minced garlic

1 tablespoon chopped parsley

Kosher salt

Freshly ground black pepper

4 skinless salmon fillets, 6 to 8 ounces each

6 ounces Brie, thinly sliced

Preheat the oven to 325 degrees.

In a small sauté pan, heat 1 tablespoon of the oil and sauté the crab, garlic, and parsley for 2 minutes, finishing with a little salt and pepper before setting this to the side.

Season the salmon with salt and pepper. In another pan, heat the remaining olive oil. Sauté the salmon, top side down, for 3 minutes. Turn the fillets over and place the pan in the oven for an additional 6 minutes. Remove from the oven and put 1 ounce of crabmeat on top of each piece of salmon. Place a few slices of cheese over the crab and put the pan back into the oven for an additional 2 minutes or until the cheese melts. Remove and serve.

⊁MO'S OPTIONS⊱

Not a salmon fan? Try swordfish or whiting.
And instead of Brie, blue cheese is a great option.

54

Mo'Nique

Red Velvet Cake

2¼ cups all-purpose flour, sifted

1 teaspoon salt

2 teaspoons unsweetened cocoa powder

2 ounces red food coloring (¼ cup)

2½ cups sugar

½ cup solid vegetable shortening

2 large eggs

1 cup buttermilk

1 teaspoon vanilla extract

1 teaspoon white vinegar

1 teaspoon baking soda

FROSTING

1½ cups confectioners' sugar

½ teaspoon cream of tartar (Now, listen, this is not for fish, you find it in the spice aisle)

1/8 teaspoon salt

4 egg whites (at room temperature)

Preheat the oven to 350 degrees.

Grease and flour two 9-inch cake pans. In a medium bowl, combine the flour and salt.

Put the cocoa in a small glass bowl and gradually add the food coloring, mixing to form a smooth paste.

In the bowl of an electric mixer, slowly beat the sugar into the shortening. Beat until fluffy, 4 to 5 minutes. Add the eggs one at a time, beating for about 30 seconds after each egg. Reduce the speed to slow and add the flour to the sugar mixture, followed by the buttermilk and the vanilla. Be sure to mix the ingredients thoroughly and scrape down the bowl once or twice. Then add the cocoa paste until the color of the batter is uniform, not streaked. Do not over-beat after adding the cocoa paste.

SKINNYCOOKSCAN'T Be TRUSTED

In a small bowl, combine the vinegar and baking soda until foamy. Stir the mixture with a spoon, then fold it into the cake batter with a wooden spoon or spatula. Pour the batter into the cake pans and bake for 25 to 30 minutes, until the top springs back to the touch. Remove and cool completely before frosting.

To make the frosting, combine the sugar, cream of tartar, salt, and ½ cup of water in a medium saucepan. Cook over medium heat, stirring, until the mixture runs clear.

In the bowl of an electric mixer, beat the egg whites until foamy. Let the mixer continue to run and slowly pour the sugar mixture in along the wall of the bowl (not into the middle). Continue beating until the egg whites are firm (do not overbeat) and the frosting is to your desired thickness. Check the frosting for sweetness. You can add more confectioners' sugar if you like.

To assemble, turn the cake layers out of the pans and set the first layer on a serving plate. Frost the top of the first layer and place the second cake layer on top of that. Finish frosting the entire cake. Chill the cake in the refrigerator before serving to stiffen the frosting a little, making it easier to cut those perfect-looking pieces.

⇥MO'S OPTIONS⇤

If you like walnuts, by all means add chopped walnuts (about 3/4 cup) to the frosting before spreading. If this damn recipe is too time-consuming, baby, I understand. Buy yourself a cream-cheese frosting and use that.

Mo'Nique

The
PERFECT ONE-POT PLEASER

Oh, how I love beef. Let me count the ways. There are ever-so-succulent short ribs, the forever fabulous filet mignon, big, bountiful, beautiful burgers, robust prime rib roasts, and one of my all-time favorites—slow-braised oxtails. Talk about some good eatin'. Next to crab and hot wings, oxtails are on my Top Ten list.

Growing up, though, oxtails weren't one of my mother's specialties. That was something we'd get from West Indian restaurants. She did make a great steak, though, and whenever we had it, you could pretty much count on my brother Steve and me to fight over who was gonna get the fat piece of meat. Now, before you go to gaspin' and sayin' how bad fat meat is for you, let me just say that I'm not encouraging folks to make a habit of eating fatty meat. But this book is about no damn substitutes, right? Well then, I'm just keepin' it real—I love the fat in meat. And every once in a while, there ain't nothing wrong with the fat meat. My motto is, "Everything in moderation—but nothing is off-limits." It's the fat, after all, that gives meat flavor and y'all know flavor, like fat, is one of my favorite words.

There's no better smell than walking into the house and getting a whiff of a pot filled with oxtails, especially after they've been simmering for hours. Just to lift the lid and take in the marriage of the meat and vegetables is tantamount to good sex. You just can't get enough. That's why, whenever I'm on the road and land in a new town, I'll have the driver take me to the most popular West Indian spot in the city. And that's usually what they are: hole-in-the-wall spots that serve some of the best food.

Over the years, Steve and I have grown to love oxtails so much that my sister-in-law,

Kelly, began making them. I gotta tell you, girlfriend puts her foot in them. This Perfect One-Pot Pleaser features my beloved oxtails in a slow-cooked stew with potatoes, onions, and carrots.

Now, some folks fuss about all the sucking that goes into getting that little bit of meat off oxtail bones. For them, it isn't worth the hassle. But I beg to differ. Baby, this is one of the tastiest fall-off-the-bone meats you can eat and worth every bit of the work that goes into it. Oh, and ladies, think of the bone-sucking as a wonderful exercise that will feed the body while also strengthening a few other necessary skills, if you know what I mean.

Mo'Nique

Oxtail Stew with Potatoes, Carrots, and Onions

Serves 4

3 to 4 pounds oxtails

1 teaspoon salt

1 teaspoon garlic salt

1 teaspoon seasoning salt

1 teaspoon freshly ground black pepper

1 cup all-purpose flour

3 tablespoons plus ¼ cup canola oil

2 large Idaho potatoes, peeled and chopped

1 (28-ounce) can whole plum tomatoes, roughly chopped, optional

½ cup chopped carrots

½ cup chopped celery

½ cup chopped onion

6 cups chicken stock

Preheat the oven to 350 degrees.

Rinse the oxtails and dry with paper towels. Season on all sides with half the seasonings. Pat the seasonings into the meat to seal in the flavor. Dredge the oxtails in the flour and shake off the excess. Place a deep cast-iron or enamel pot over a high flame and heat the 3 tablespoons of canola oil. Sear the oxtails until browned on both sides. Add the potatoes and the chopped plum tomatoes (if you are using them), and take off the heat.

In a separate sauté pan, heat the ¼ cup of canola oil. Add the carrots, celery, onions, and remaining seasonings, and quickly sauté. Remove from the heat and scrape everything into the pot with the oxtails. Add the chicken stock, cover, and slide the pot into the oven and let it cook for 1½ to 2 hours.

⊱MO'S TIP⊰

Using a Crock-Pot is an excellent—and easy—way to achieve a tender oxtail stew, especially if you put it on before heading out the door for work. Use only 4 cups of stock or it will be too soupy. When you get home, dinner's ready.

Bahama
MAMA

I discovered the beauty of the Bahamas when my travel agent, Raschinna, booked me at the Atlantis Resort on Nassau's Paradise Island. After that, I began to rent houses and was close to buying one until a native (a rather fine gentleman, Burton) told me I might enjoy the unspoiled nature of his hometown, Great Exuma, and invited me over for a few days.

He was right.

Unlike the more popular—and populated—Nassau, Exuma consists of two main islands: Great Exuma and Little Exuma, located thirty-five miles southeast of Nassau. It's the kind of place unconcerned with time schedules and with who the hell Miss Parker is. On Great Exuma, everyone knows one another; folks are friendly. They wave as they pass. There's one bridge into town that overlooks Elizabeth Harbour, and the mesmerizing, turquoise waters of the Atlantic are crystal clear. I've often said that if this is what heaven is like, I look forward to it. Here, the people treat me like a long-lost sister.

And you can usually find this sister behind the outdoor bar mixing up drinks for the locals at Two Turtles Inn, a small, family-owned hotel on Main Street. My friend's family has owned the inn for years. Now, Two Turtles isn't a fancy place. In fact, there are only fourteen rooms in the entire resort and that's what I dig about it. It's the ideal place to spend lazy afternoons lounging, laughing, listening to lively steel drum music, and enjoying out-of-this-world Bahamian food prepared by the matriarch of Two Turtles, Miss Pat, who hooks up some of the best pigeon peas and rice and okra stew I've ever tasted.

I was so impressed with the island and the people that I made a commitment to assist them by keeping the one grocery store (which was grossly overpriced) stocked with staples as a way of giving back to the beautiful people there. So, if you hear that Mo'Nique has retired and moved away, you can probably find me chillin' on the beach in Exuma with my children running around as I lie back and swing on a hammock, sipping a cocktail while overlooking the peaceful Atlantic.

Now, I know there's a distinct difference between the Bahamas and Jamaica, but many of the dishes are similar and it's not easy to find Bahamian food in the States. To this day, whenever I land in a city, I'll ask the driver to take me to the best West Indian restaurant before we head to the hotel. Two of my favorites: Negril in Washington, D.C., and Harlem's Pepper Pot. I discovered Negril while working as a morning deejay at WHUR, Howard University's on-campus radio station. It's one of those take-it-and-go spots, which is fine with me, because I like to get comfortable and savor the flavors in the comfort of my suite. The Pepper Pot is a must when visiting the Big Apple. (I found it while taping episodes of *It's Showtime at the Apollo.*)

The key to good jerk is in the spice. This one isn't for those with delicate stomachs.

Mo'Nique

Jerk Chicken

5 pounds chicken, cut into serving pieces

2 cups white vinegar, plus 1 teaspoon

2 tablespoons soy sauce

Juice of 2 limes (¼ cup)

2 bay leaves

6 garlic cloves, minced (about 1 tablespoon)

2 cups finely chopped green onions

1 Scotch bonnet, seeded and minced (Wear gloves 'cause these peppers are hot!)

1 tablespoon salt

2 teaspoons sugar

1½ teaspoons dried thyme, crumbled

1 teaspoon ground cinnamon

5 teaspoons ground allspice

Jerk Chicken
Jamaican Barbecue Sauce
Jamaican Rice and Peas
Braised Cabbage
Bread Pudding
Serves 4

63

Rinse the chicken pieces well in 2 cups of vinegar, drain, and set aside. Whisk together or pulse briefly in a food processor the teaspoon of vinegar and the rest of the ingredients. Reserve 2 tablespoons of this marinade for the Jamaican Barbecue Sauce.

Rinse the chicken pieces well under cold running water and pat dry with paper towels. Put the chicken into 2 heavy-duty plastic sealable bags and divide the marinade evenly between them. Turn the bags over to distribute the marinade, and refrigerate the chicken for at least 24 hours and up to 2 days. Turn the bags over occasionally to redistribute the marinade.

About an hour before you plan to serve the chicken, prepare a charcoal fire. Take the chicken out of the marinade, discarding any leftover marinade. On an oiled grill rack set about 6 inches above red-hot coals, grill the chicken (in batches if necessary), covered, for 10 to 15 minutes on each side, until cooked through. Transfer to a warm platter and keep warm under tented foil until serving. Serve with Jamaican Barbecue Sauce (recipe follows).

Jamaican Barbecue Sauce

1¼ cups ketchup

⅓ cup soy sauce

2 tablespoons Jamaican hot pepper sauce

2 tablespoons jerk marinade (reserved from recipe on page 63)

3 green onions, minced

3 garlic cloves, minced

3 tablespoons fresh minced ginger

⅓ cup dark brown sugar

⅓ cup white vinegar

3 tablespoons dark rum

In a medium nonstick saucepan, combine all the ingredients except the rum and bring to a boil, stirring to dissolve the sugar. Reduce the heat and simmer for about 12 minutes, until the sauce is thick, flavorful, and coats the back of a spoon. Remove from the heat and stir in the rum. Cool the sauce to room temperature before serving. This makes about 2 cups and will keep, refrigerated, for 4 to 5 days.

⊱MO'S OPTIONS⊰

If you don't have time to make the sauce from scratch, try one of my favorites, Spicy Caribbee Jerk Rub (www.spicycaribbee.com). Substitute 2 cups of Spicy Caribbee for the Jerk Chicken marinade. You can also bake the chicken in the oven at 325 to 350 degrees for about 35 minutes.

⊱MO'S TIP⊰

Before you tackle this menu, have plenty of water nearby because jerk ain't no joke, baby. Understand that if it's hot going in—need I say more?

Mo'Nique

Jamaican Rice and Peas

1½ cups dried red kidney beans, picked over and rinsed

2 garlic cloves, crushed

Salt

½ cup unsweetened coconut milk

2 green onions, chopped

1 teaspoon thyme

1 Scotch bonnet or habanero chile, diced (wear gloves when handling hot chiles)

2 cups long-grain white rice

Freshly ground black pepper

The night before cooking, fill a container with cold water and add the beans. Cover and soak overnight.

Bring 4 quarts of water to a boil in a large pot. Add the beans, the garlic and a generous pinch of salt. Simmer until the beans are tender, about 1½ hours. Strain the beans, reserving 3 cups of the cooking liquid. Place the beans and the reserved liquid back in the pot along with the coconut milk, onions, thyme, and chile. Bring to a boil and add the rice. Season with salt and pepper. Cover and let simmer for 20 minutes, until all the water has been absorbed. Stir it with a wooden spoon before serving.

⊁MO'S OPTION⊱

If you want to save time, use canned beans instead of dried ones, and reduce cooking time accordingly.

Braised Cabbage

2 heads green cabbage

¼ cup olive oil

1 yellow bell pepper, seeded and sliced

1 teaspoon minced garlic

2 tablespoons butter

4 cups chicken stock

Salt and freshly ground black pepper

Remove the outer leaves of the cabbage. Cut the cabbage in half, core, and shred as for cole-slaw. Wash thoroughly and drain. Heat the olive oil in a large pot over a high flame and sauté the bell pepper. Add the cabbage, garlic, butter, and chicken stock and season with salt and pepper. Cover and simmer for 9 to 12 minutes, stirring occasionally, until the cabbage is tender. Check the seasoning and serve.

Mo'Nique

Bread Pudding

10 cups sourdough bread, cubed

½ cup unsalted butter, melted

3 large eggs

1 cup sugar

1 quart heavy cream

2 tablespoons Grand Marnier

2 teaspoons vanilla extract

1 teaspoon hazelnut extract

1½ teaspoons ground nutmeg

1½ teaspoons ground cinnamon

Preheat the oven to 350 degrees.

Place the bread cubes in a baking dish and pour the butter over them and toss. In a large bowl, whisk together the remaining ingredients and pour the mixture over the buttered bread. Bake, uncovered, for 45 to 50 minutes, until a light golden brown. If you desire a darker, firmer bread pudding, cook a few minutes longer.

⋇MO'S OPTIONS⋇

Caramel sauce, caramelized walnuts, or fresh fruit make great toppings.

⋇MO'S BEVERAGE⋇

I love the flavor of Malibu rum. To get your island spice on, mix 3 parts Coca-Cola with 1 part Malibu rum coconut (more if you really want to get nice), and serve over ice.

Home
FOR THE HOLIDAYS

Of all the holidays, Thanksgiving is probably my favorite. Despite a hectic schedule that typically has me on the road doing stand-up most of the year, holidays included, I look forward to slowing down and being home at Thanksgiving and Christmas with my family, especially now that I have little ones. It's also a time to reflect on the year and to give thanks for all of my blessings.

Back in the day, my mother, Miss Alice, always seemed to love fixing the holiday dinners, but these days, when that time of year rolls around, she starts dropping hints about how she isn't going to fix the entire meal. And she comes up with all kinds of reasons why. We've heard everything from she doesn't want to go broke shopping for food (we'll provide the money), doesn't have time (she's retired), and doesn't feel like it to she's taught us all to make her specialties—which is true. And though my sister, Millicent, and I make her macaroni and cheese and collard greens well, this is the one time of year where we don't want any mistakes. So, it only makes sense that Miss Alice does the cooking. And I know making the holiday meals is no easy job these days, because there are usually no less than fifteen of us.

In addition to traditional Thanksgiving fare like turkey, ham, yams, and macaroni and cheese, there are also family favorites like rabbit, seafood salad, oxtails, corn pudding, and collard greens. And no holiday table is complete without mom's signature Orange Roughy Topped with Crabmeat, which always takes center stage. (One year, baby she must've been in a rush, because the fish blew up in the oven. Don't think she didn't serve it, anyway. We ate every bit of it, too.)

One of my fondest Thanksgivings was 2005. The twins had just come home from the hospital and we were gearing up for dinner at my house. Millicent and I were going over the menu with my mother, and every time we asked her what she planned to bring, she'd try to get out of making anything. I guess she figured she'd sit back and let us handle it, but to us, it just isn't the holidays if Miss Alice doesn't contribute.

"I'm telling y'all, I'm not making the entire meal," she crowed.

"Fine. I'll make the dressing. Millicent, you make the greens. Mom, you make the macaroni and cheese, the rabbit, and your stuffed fish," I said.

"You and Millicent know how to make the macaroni and cheese."

"I know, but, Ma, you always put your foot in it."

"Well, how long am I gonna have to make it?" she asked.

"Until you die," I blurted out. "Then we'll take over."

Now, I don't know where that came from and surely that's not a nice thing to say to your mother. I didn't mean to tell her to cook for us until she dies. It just slipped out. And all the three of us could do was laugh because as much as she hates doing it, it just isn't the holidays without our mother's cooking. Her contribution, or lack thereof, wasn't the end of the laughter that year.

That day, folks were famished. We hurriedly put the dishes on the table and gathered around so my father could bless the food. As he made his way into the circle, we all bowed our heads and prepared for a heartfelt prayer. You know how Thanksgiving prayers drag on in some black families, they're like church sermons; folks are nearly falling out trying to make it through them. Well, not in my family and not with my father. He eyed all that good food, closed his eyes, and uttered, "thank you" and was done. No "bless the food and the hands that prepared it." No "thank you for family and good friends." Just, "thank you." Baby, that's got to go down as the shortest prayer in the history of Thanksgiving prayers. Right up there with, "Jesus wept." After a few moments of silence thinking there was more to come, we all opened our eyes to see if he was finished. He was already reaching for a piece of turkey.

It's funny moments like these, and helping to prepare menus filled with all of our favorites, that make holidays so special. Here's the Imes family menu. Enjoy!

Mo'Nique

Orange Roughy Topped with Crabmeat

1 pound lump crabmeat, picked over for shells and cartilage

3 tablespoons mayonnaise

2 tablespoons Dijon mustard

2 tablespoons Old Bay seasoning

1 tablespoon Worcestershire sauce

2 tablespoons Louisiana-style hot sauce

2 tablespoons chopped flat-leaf parsley

2 tablespoons olive oil

4 skinless orange roughy fillets, 6 to 8 ounces each

Salt and freshly ground black pepper

¼ cup bread crumbs

Paprika, optional

Orange Roughy Topped with Crabmeat
Braised Rabbit
Fried Chicken (page 5)
Cornbread Dressing
Crab Balls (page 100)
Pigs' Tails
Yams
Corn Casserole
Green Beans with Onion, Bacon, and Butter (page 91)
Cranberry Sauce (see Mo's Tips page 77)
Sweet Potato Pie
Pound Cake
Serves 4

71

Preheat the oven to 350 degrees.

Mix the crabmeat with the mayonnaise, mustard, Old Bay seasoning, Worcestershire, hot sauce, and half of the parsley. Cover and refrigerate until ready to use, up to one day.

In an ovenproof sauté pan, heat the oil over high flame. Season both sides of the fish with salt and pepper, and lay the fillets into the hot oil. Cook on each side for 2 minutes. Remove the pan from the heat and spread 2 tablespoons of the crab mixture over the top of each fillet. Top with a sprinkling of the bread crumbs and paprika, if using. Bake the fish for 7 to 10 minutes. (If you don't have an ovenproof sauté pan, transfer the fillets to a baking pan before putting them in the oven.) The crab should be nice and hot, and the bread crumbs brown. Sprinkle with the remaining parsley and serve.

⊁MO'S OPTIONS⊱

Miss Alice tops the fish with a package of Knorr hollandaise sauce made per the package instructions (but with milk instead of water and with the addition of one stick of butter). Prepare the fish as above and pour the sauce over the fish before serving it. If orange roughy isn't available in your area, or if it isn't to your taste, swordfish is great, too.

Mo'Nique

Braised Rabbit

1 cup plus 1 tablespoon all-purpose flour

2 teaspoons seasoning salt

2 teaspoons salt

2 teaspoons freshly ground black pepper

2 rabbits, about 2½ pounds each, cut in serving pieces (your butcher can do this)

1 cup vegetable oil

1 tablespoon butter

1 large white onion, chopped

2 cups chicken stock

Mix the cup of flour with the salts and the pepper, and thoroughly coat the pieces of rabbit. In a medium pot, heat the oil over a high flame. Shake off any excess flour, lay the rabbit into the oil, and brown on all sides. Do this in batches if necessary. Remove the rabbit from the pot and set aside on a plate.

Pour off and discard the excess oil, leaving a few tablespoons in the pot. Add the butter and the tablespoon of flour. Cook over low heat, incorporating the browned bits left from cooking the meat, until the mixture reaches a rich brown color. Add the onions, chicken stock, and 1 cup of water. Season the liquid with salt and pepper and add the rabbit back into the pot. Simmer, covered, for about 1 hour.

73

Cornbread Dressing

1 recipe cornbread (page 8)

1 tablespoon bacon fat, plus ½ cup, optional

1 Vidalia onion, diced

2 celery stalks, diced

½ teaspoon dried sage

2 cups chicken stock

1 egg, beaten

Salt and freshly ground black pepper

4 green onions, white part only, chopped

Preheat the oven to 350 degrees.

Crumble the cornbread into a large bowl. In a sauté pan, heat the 1 tablespoon bacon fat over a high flame and sauté the onion and celery for about 5 minutes. Add the mixture to the cornbread, followed by the sage and the ½ cup bacon fat, if you're including this. Mix well, then add the chicken stock, egg, salt and pepper, and green onions. Grease a 2- to 3-quart baking dish and pour in the dressing. Bake for 25 to 40 minutes, until golden brown and all the liquid has been absorbed. (To see if it's done, stick a small knife or toothpick into the center of the dressing. If it comes out clean and dry, it's ready to come out.)

Mo'Nique

Pigs' Tails

8 to 10 pigs' tails

1 tablespoon salt

1 tablespoon seasoning salt

1 tablespoon garlic salt

1 tablespoon cracked black peppercorns

1 cup bacon fat

2 white onions, roughly chopped

6 garlic cloves, crushed

1 bay leaf

2 (15-ounce) cans sauerkraut, drained

Wash the tails, pat dry, and place in a bowl. Toss with the salts and peppercorns until completely coated. Heat the bacon fat in a stockpot on high flame. Sauté the onions and pigs' tails briefly. Add the garlic and the bay leaf and water to cover. Bring to a low simmer and cook for 60 to 90 minutes. Check the meat for doneness; it should be tender enough to fall off the bone. Add the sauerkraut to the pot. Simmer for another 15 to 20 minutes to allow the seasoning to infuse the sauerkraut. Discard the bay leaf and serve each portion of meat with some of the sauerkraut.

Yams

4 to 6 yams, peeled and cut into medium-size chunks

½ cup light brown sugar

½ cup granulated sugar

1 tablespoon ground cinnamon

2 teaspoons ground nutmeg

6 tablespoons unsalted butter

1 tablespoon vanilla extract

Place the yams into a deep saucepan. In a bowl, mix the dry ingredients and add to the pan, followed by the butter, vanilla, and 1½ cups water. Cover the pot and bring up to a medium heat, simmering for 15 to 25 minutes. Check after the first 10 minutes, mix well, and continue to cook until the yams are soft.

Mo'Nique

Corn Casserole

3 (15-ounce) cans whole kernel corn, drained

2 (15-ounce) cans cream-style corn

½ cup (1 stick) butter, melted

3 large eggs

1 cup sugar

1 tablespoon flour

½ teaspoon vanilla

Preheat the oven to 350 degrees. Place all the ingredients in a bowl and stir well. Pour into an ovenproof casserole and bake for 30 to 35 minutes until nearly set in the center. Serve hot.

❈MO'S TIP❈

For the cranberry sauce, take it easy and use canned!
Chill and serve in a cut-glass bowl.

77

Sweet Potato Pie

1 (9-inch) unbaked pie crust

4 large sweet potatoes

6 tablespoons unsalted butter

1¼ cups granulated sugar

2 large eggs

¼ cup milk

1 teaspoon vanilla extract

2 teaspoons ground allspice

1 teaspoon honey

Light brown sugar

Preheat the oven to 325 degrees.

Using a fork, prick holes in the bottom of the pie crust. Place in the oven for 1 minute, remove, and set aside.

Peel the sweet potatoes and place them in a large pot with cold water to cover. Bring to a boil and cook for about 30 minutes, or until soft. Drain. Transfer the potatoes to the bowl of an electric mixer. On medium speed, beat the potatoes until smooth. Add the butter, granulated sugar, eggs, milk, vanilla, and allspice, and beat to combine. Add the honey, mix well, and pour the mixture into the pie shell. Bake for 1 hour until set. Finish it with a sprinkle of brown sugar over the top when it comes out of the oven.

⊱MO'S OPTION⊰

Top with Cool Whip and a dash of ground cinnamon.

Mo'Nique

Pound Cake

1½ cups unsalted butter, plus 1 tablespoon for buttering the pan

1 (8-ounce) package cream cheese, at room temperature

3 cups granulated sugar

1 teaspoon vanilla extract

1 teaspoon almond extract

1 teaspoon lemon extract

6 large eggs

3 cups cake flour

1 teaspoon light brown sugar, optional

Preheat the oven to 325 degrees and grease a loaf pan with the 1 tablespoon butter.

In the bowl of an electric mixer, beat the cream cheese, granulated sugar, and butter until there are no lumps. Add the vanilla, the almond and the lemon extracts, and beat in the eggs, one at a time. Once this is all combined, add in the flour and mix until the batter is smooth.

Pour the batter into the prepared pan and bake for 1½ hours. A few minutes before the cake is done, sprinkle the brown sugar, if using, on top, then return to the oven to finish baking.

⊰MO'S TIP⊱

This menu is for all the fixings that go along with your holiday bird. If you don't have time to prepare a turkey, or if you prefer a fried bird, Jive Turkey, in Brooklyn, New York, offers succulent fried turkeys in a variety of flavors and will ship them to you overnight (www.thejiveturkey.com).

Brunch
FIT FOR A QUEEN

I'm willing to bet that the concept of the all-you-can-eat brunch was invented by a F.A.T. gal. Who could come up with a brilliant idea like paying one price and eating to your heart's content, except someone who thoroughly enjoys food?

When I was growing up, brunches were reserved for Sundays—you know, after that marathon church service. But these days, you can find them just about anywhere, any day, and at any hour. In addition to popular spots like HomeTown Buffet (with locations all over the United States), it isn't hard to find some sort of all-you-can-eat salad, seafood, or dessert bar. But nobody beats the eats and treats you can find at the brunches served in Las Vegas. Baby, they take the cake. It's the land of buffets and lavish brunches. And the beauty of the Vegas brunch is that even for a Big Girl like me, it's impossible to sample all of the endless assortment of omelets, steaks, seafood, salads, fruits, cheeses, and desserts that are there for the taking. In Vegas, it's excess at its tasty best. That's why you better run if you happen upon one of those order-off-the-menu brunches. That's fake brunch and it ain't for me. I like options—lots of them. This brunch menu, though it isn't big, offers a nice mix of items that are sure to please.

Crabmeat Omelet

1 Hass avocado

1 plum tomato

2 green onions, green part only

1 tablespoon olive oil

6 large eggs

2 tablespoons cream

1 tablespoon unsalted butter

Pinch of salt

Pinch of white pepper

4 ounces lump crabmeat

4 ounces mozzarella cheese (or Cheddar if you like)

Pinch of paprika

Crabmeat Omelet
Hash Browns
Buttermilk Waffles
Grand Marnier Syrup
Sausage (see Mo's Tips, page 85)
Mixed Berry Salad
Strawberry, Kiwi, and Mango Smoothie
Serves 4

82

Cut the avocado and tomato into small dice, and thinly slice the green onions, setting all to the side. In a large sauté pan, heat the olive oil over low heat. Crack the eggs into a bowl and beat until smooth, add the cream, and mix well. Once the pan is hot, add the butter. Once it is melted, add the eggs, salt, and pepper. Stir until the eggs begin to set, 2 minutes. Spread the avocado, tomato, half of the crabmeat, and half of the mozzarella over one half of the eggs. Let everything cook for 2 minutes more. Using a heatproof rubber spatula, fold the omelet in half, closing up the omelet around the filling. Cook for 30 seconds on one side, turn it over, and cook for 30 seconds more. Slide the omelet out of the pan onto a warm platter. Garnish with the remaining crabmeat and cheese, and a dash of paprika.

Hash Browns

4 medium Idaho potatoes, peeled

1½ tablespoons olive oil

2 tablespoons finely chopped Vidalia onions

1 small garlic clove, minced

2 green onions, chopped

Salt and freshly ground white or black pepper

Fill a large bowl with cold water. Shred the potatoes with a grater and place in the water to prevent discoloring.

Heat a skillet over high flame for about 60 seconds. Add the olive oil, onions, garlic, and green onions and sauté. Add the potatoes, toss to mix well, and season with the salt and pepper. Cook for 4 to 6 minutes, until golden brown, then flip and cook on the other side for another 4 to 6 minutes. Test the hash browns for doneness. Serve hot right from the pan.

Buttermilk Waffles

6 large eggs

2 cups buttermilk

2 sticks butter, melted

1¼ cups sifted flour

1½ teaspoons baking soda

1½ teaspoons baking powder

½ pint (1 cup) fresh strawberries, stemmed

Heat a waffle iron and spray with nonstick cooking spray. Beat the eggs, buttermilk, and melted butter in a large bowl. Slowly add the sifted flour, stirring until smooth. Stir in the baking soda and baking powder, mixing thoroughly. Pour in enough batter to fill the waffle maker completely. Close the lid. Cook until the waffle maker indicates completion, or until the waffle is golden brown on the outside. To check doneness, stick a toothpick into the center of the waffle; it should come out clean. Serve the waffles with the strawberries and Grand Marnier Syrup (recipe follows).

Mo'Nique

Grand Marnier Syrup

1 (30-ounce) bottle Mrs. Butterworth's syrup

2 cups Grand Marnier liqueur (see Mo's Tips)

2 teaspoons vanilla syrup

1 teaspoon lemon juice

1 tablespoon grated orange zest

1 teaspoon ground cinnamon

Pour the syrup into a medium saucepan and bring to a simmer over low heat. Once the syrup is simmering, add the Grand Marnier, vanilla syrup, lemon juice, orange zest, and cinnamon. Mix well and serve hot.

✳ MO'S TIPS ✳

If you're serving this to little ones, eliminate the Grand Marnier. If you're trying to go for round two (or three, or four) with your honey, then add more.
And if I have to tell you how to make sausage, baby, you have problems I can't handle. I'm playing with you. Just follow the directions on the package of your favorite one.

Mixed Berry Salad

5 medium strawberries, stemmed

1 pint raspberries

1 pint blueberries

1 pint blackberries

Small bunch of fresh mint

½ cup vanilla syrup, optional

Wash all of the berries and drain them well. Halve or quarter the strawberries if they are large and place in a medium bowl with the rest of the berries. Remove the mint leaves from the stems and add them to the bowl. Add half the vanilla syrup and toss to coat. Before serving, pour the remaining syrup over the top. Garnish with a small sprig of mint.

Mo'Nique

Strawberry, Kiwi, and Mango Smoothie

1 cup pineapple juice

3 kiwis, peeled

1 mango, peeled

1 cup banana slices (about 2 bananas)

3/4 cup whole frozen strawberries

Place all the ingredients in a blender. Blend on low (make sure the lid is secure) for about 1 minute. Switch to high and blend until smooth.

87

Rita's
SECRET SUPPER

I've got a homegirl, Rita, who may have missed her true calling in life. Though she's a fine hairdresser, Rita's an even more wonderful cook who could easily have become a gourmet chef. I met Rita back in Baltimore through a cousin and we've kept in touch over the years. I didn't know just how good a cook Rita was until she agreed to become my full-time hairdresser, which meant she had to move into my home. With my hectic schedule, I never know when I'm going to need my hair hooked up. Baby, in between weaving, glueing, pressing, twisting, and braiding hair, Miss Rita will have a pot of collard greens simmering on the stove, a roast cooking in the oven, and a cake waiting to be frosted. And the thing I dig about this sister is that for her, cooking is a joy just like tellin' jokes is for me. She can whip up a superb meal, often from scratch, in no time flat. Every night, there's something different to try. One night she was experimenting and made some egg foo yong that tasted like it came straight from a Chinese restaurant.

But there's one thing that irks Rita to no end and that's when folks ask her how to make one of her delicious dishes, or hover for clues when she's working her magic. As a connoisseur of good food, I was dying to know some of her secrets, especially since she was whipping them up in my kitchen. But trying to get her to divulge her culinary secrets is like trying to get the CIA to give up the whereabouts of Osama bin Laden. It ain't happenin'. All she'll say is "It's a secret. Don't worry about it. Just enjoy it." So, I do. Every chance I get.

Everyone is born with a gift and Rita's is cooking. And as all good cooks know, to achieve wonderful results, you don't have to season food to death. Though it was tough, I convinced Rita to give up her recipe for simple baked chicken. The beauty of this one—and of Rita's cooking—is that there isn't anything tricky to it. It's definitely a crowd pleaser.

Baked Garlic and Basil Chicken

1 whole chicken, about 3 pounds

2 sprigs fresh rosemary

2 sprigs fresh thyme

Handful of fresh basil leaves

3 to 4 large garlic cloves, roughly chopped (1 tablespoon)

¼ cup olive oil

2 teaspoons salt

2 teaspoons garlic salt

1 teaspoon seasoning salt

1 teaspoon freshly ground white pepper

1 teaspoon paprika

**Baked Garlic and Basil Chicken
Green Beans with Onion, Bacon, and Butter
Potatoes au Gratin
Serves 4**

90

Preheat the oven to 325 degrees.

Remove the innards of the chicken and save (if you like). Wash the chicken in cold water and pat dry with paper towels. Stem the rosemary and thyme, and add to a blender along with the basil, garlic, and half of the olive oil. Blend together to make a rub. Season the chicken with the salts, pepper, and paprika, and rub the herb mixture all over. Fold the wings under the back of the bird and tie the legs together.

Pour the remaining olive oil in the bottom of a medium baking pan, add the chicken, and bake for 45 minutes. Rotate the chicken every 12 to 15 minutes until it is golden brown, cooked through, and juicy.

⇥ MO'S OPTIONS ⇤

If you prefer, this dish can be made with cut-up fryers or chicken parts.

Mo'Nique

Green Beans with Onion, Bacon, and Butter

3 to 4 pounds fresh green beans

I pound sliced bacon

I large Vidalia onion, chopped

4 garlic cloves, smashed

Kosher salt

Juice of I lemon

3 tablespoons salted butter

Freshly ground black pepper

Cut the ends off the green beans (or snap them like the old folks did and remove the string). Wash and drain the beans. Cut the bacon into small cubes, and set it aside with the onion and garlic, until ready to use.

Bring a large pot of salted water to a boil (about 2 tablespoons salt to 1½ gallons of water). Add the beans and the lemon juice. Let this boil gently for 7 to 10 minutes, until the beans are tender. Drain the beans, reserving about 2 cups of the cooking water.

In a large sauté pan, cook the bacon. Then add the onion and garlic. Sauté for 7 to 10 minutes over low heat. Add the beans and the reserved water to the bacon mixture. Add the butter, season with salt and pepper, and cover. Simmer for 5 minutes over low heat. Serve.

Potatoes au Gratin

6 to 7 medium Idaho potatoes (3 pounds)

2 tablespoons unsalted butter, softened, for buttering the baking dish

3 medium garlic cloves, crushed through a garlic press or minced

1½ cups milk

Salt and freshly ground black pepper

Freshly grated nutmeg

⅓ cup heavy cream

4 tablespoons crème fraîche, optional

¼ cup grated Parmesan cheese

Preheat the oven to 350 degrees.

Peel and wash the potatoes, and slice them into rounds ⅛ inch thick.

Generously butter a heavy, shallow baking dish, preferably earthenware or enameled cast iron (or a large cast-iron skillet). Rub the dish with half of the crushed garlic. In a small saucepan, bring the milk to a simmer with the remaining garlic and season with salt and pepper. Set aside.

Arrange some of the potatoes in one overlapping layer on the bottom of the dish. Season the layer generously with salt, pepper, and nutmeg. Continue layering the potatoes, seasoning each layer liberally. You may not need all the potatoes. Press the layers down to compress them. Pour in enough of the milk to come up just a little below the top layer of potatoes. Cover the baking dish with foil, set it on a larger baking sheet, and bake it until the potatoes feel tender when pierced with a knife, about 1 hour.

Mo'Nique

and he does it so well) deals each player two cards. The first player up reveals his ha[nd] says, "I wanna get in between," and places a bet. Now, you can bet as little or as much [as you] want, even the entire pot, if you've got the money to cover it. The dealer then deals a [third] card. If the card falls in between the two original cards dealt, then you win the amount [you] bet. If you get a card that's the same as one of your original cards, or that's larger or smal[ler,] you lose. So, let's say I'm dealt a one and a ten. I decide to bet $40 that I'll get a number b[e-] tween those and tell the dealer to deal me a third card. He deals a six. I win $40 out of th[e] pot. Sounds easy, right? Well, this particular time, I got an ace (the highest card in the deck) and a two (the lowest card in the deck) which meant that unless I got another ace or two, I couldn't lose. The pot was at $2,500 and in order to win it, I had to put up $2,500. The problem was, I only had $600, which meant that's all I could win. Already, I'm trying to come up with a creative way to get the additional $1,900. But you can't leave the table, there's no running to the ATM, or writing IOUs. It's either put it up right then and there, or too bad for you. Now, it was hard to see all that money in front of me, knowing it could be mine. This is why I love Vette. She sensed I was in trouble and started to kick me under the table to let me know she would go upstairs and front me the $1,900. But I was laughing so much and was so full (in more ways than one) that I wasn't catching her hints, especially with girlfriend's famous apple pie (with extra crust, just the way I like it) calling my name. Instead of holdin' out, I put up the $600, made $1,200, and then made my way over to the pie. When food distracts you from money, you know it has to be good.

You'll notice that most of the dishes on this menu feature some sort of sauce. There's a reason for that—the sauce helps mark the cards.

This menu features three of my favorites: buffalo wings, crab cakes, and Yvette's famous apple pie with lots of crust!

Raise the oven temperature to 425 degrees, remove the foil, and bake until the top begins to brown, about 10 minutes. Pour just enough of the heavy cream to cover the top and dab it with crème fraîche, if using. (Crème fraîche is a thickened, slightly tangy cream that lends a mellow smoothness to sauces.) Sprinkle the Parmesan evenly over the potatoes. Bake until the top is brown and bubbly, another 15 to 20 minutes. Remove from the oven and let the potatoes stand for 10 minutes to absorb the cream. Cut into squares and serve.

⇥MO'S OPTIONS⇤

Betty Crocker cheesy Cheddar casserole potatoes are a delicious and quick substitute. You can easily doctor up the dish with grated Parmesan or Cheddar and some finely sliced green onions.

Card
PARTY GET-DOWN

I told you earlier that Mo'Nique's, my comedy joint in Baltimore, was a hot spot for laughs and good food, like our signature Mo Burger, right? Well, I neglected to mention another popular dish: our slap-somebody-in-the-mouth-'cause-these-are-the-best-I've-ever-tasted chicken wings. You could get them all kinds of ways: simply fried, slathered in barbecue sauce, dipped in a honey mustard concoction, Buffalo-style with plenty of hot sauce, or as a combo with a little of each. I don't know what it is about black folks (count me as one of them) and that particular piece of bird, but folks just couldn't get enough—and I never have, either.

When I'm in the mood to talk loud, eat well, and have a good old-fashioned card party, wings are always on the menu. Whether the game of choice is spades or bid whist, every time is a good time when I get together with my friend (and *Parkers* costar) Yvette Wilson. Like me, Vette (as we call her) began as a stand-up comedienne, but what most people may not know is that in addition to being a great actress, girlfriend is also a wonderful cook. We're talking professional chef material. Like me, Yvette and her husband, Jerome, love to entertain. Whenever we get together at their home, there's always plenty of drinks, jokes, good food, and laughs to go around, especially when the cards come out and we get to playing—and cheating at—a game called "in between." Most folks play for fun, but not this crowd—we place cash bets that range anywhere from 25¢ to $2,500. Things usually start out cool, until folks get to eatin', drinkin', and lyin'. Then all hell breaks loose.

The way the game works is that the dealer (which is always Jerome because it's his house

Buffalo Wings

4 pounds chicken wings

1 tablespoon seasoning salt

1 tablespoon garlic salt

1 tablespoon kosher salt

1 tablespoon freshly ground black pepper

2 cups canola oil

2 cups all-purpose flour

HOT SAUCE

2 bottles Red Rooster hot sauce

4 garlic cloves, crushed

2 tablespoons unsalted butter

Buffalo Wings
Jalapeño Crab Dip
Nachos with Crabmeat
Crab Balls
Vette's Apple Pie
Long Island Iced Tea
(see Mo's Beverage, page 102)
Serves 4

97

Wash the chicken wings and pat dry. Combine all of the seasonings and season the wings according to your taste. In a large sauté pan, heat the oil over a medium-high flame. Dredge the wings in the flour, coating evenly and shaking off any excess. Gently place the wings into the oil and fry for 8 to 12 minutes, turning occasionally, until cooked through and golden brown. Drain the wings on paper towels, then transfer them to a serving platter.

To make the hot sauce, in a small saucepan, combine the hot sauce, garlic, and butter. Bring the sauce to a simmer, then pour it over the wings and serve with celery sticks and your favorite blue cheese dressing.

⤞ MO'S OPTIONS ⤝

For wings with a twist, replace the hot sauce with your favorite barbecue sauce. Or try adding lemon pepper seasoning to the rub.

Jalapeño Crab Dip

2 pounds lump crabmeat, picked over for shells and cartilage

1 cup grated Jack cheese

2 tablespoons mayonnaise

¼ cup minced garlic

¼ cup grated Parmesan

1 small jalapeño, diced

2 teaspoons hot sauce

2 teaspoons Worcestershire sauce

1 teaspoon salt

1 teaspoon freshly ground black pepper

Preheat the oven to 350 degrees.

Combine all the ingredients with a fork or wooden spoon and transfer it to an ovenproof dish. Bake until nicely browned, about 20 minutes. Sprinkle with more pepper and serve with an assortment of chips.

98

⊰MO'S OPTIONS⊱

If you *really* like jalapeños, add a few after the dip comes out of the oven for an even spicier kick. You can use pickled or fresh ones, sliced or finely chopped. The seeds and inner membrane of the pepper add the fire, so use accordingly.

Mo'Nique

Nachos with Crabmeat

2 tablespoons butter, softened

2 shallots, finely chopped

8 ounces lump crabmeat, picked over for shells and cartilage

Salt and freshly ground pepper

2 plum tomatoes, diced

¼ cup diced white onion

1 jalapeño, diced

½ cup grated mozzarella

½ cup grated mild cheddar

1-pound bag corn chips

Preheat the oven to 325 degrees.

Heat the butter in a medium sauté pan. Add the shallots and crabmeat, and sauté for 3 minutes over medium heat. Season with salt and pepper. Remove from the heat and let cool while dicing the tomatoes, onions, and jalapeño, and grating the cheeses. Once everything is done, spread the chips on a medium baking pan, sprinkle the crab and the two cheeses over the top, and bake until the cheeses are melted. Top with the tomatoes, onions, and pepper and serve.

➤MO'S OPTIONS➤

A great addition to, or substitution for, the crabmeat is chopped sautéed spinach or sautéed artichokes.

Crab Balls

3 tablespoons Worcestershire sauce

2 tablespoons Dijon mustard

2 tablespoons mayonnaise

1 large egg, beaten

1 tablespoon dried parsley

2 teaspoons Old Bay seasoning

1 tablespoon cayenne pepper

2 tablespoons seasoned bread crumbs, plus 1 to 2 cups for coating the cakes

1 pound back fin (or lump) crabmeat, picked over for shells and cartilage

1 cup canola oil

In a medium bowl combine the Worcestershire sauce, mustard, mayonnaise, egg, parsley, Old Bay, cayenne, and the 2 tablespoons bread crumbs. Gently fold in the crabmeat and shape the mixture into cakes or small balls. Put the 1 to 2 cups bread crumbs into a bowl and roll the cakes in the crumbs to coat.

In a sauté pan, heat the oil and fry the cakes for 2 to 3 minutes on each side, until golden brown and hot on the inside. Place on a paper towel to absorb any excess oil. Serve with tartar sauce or rémoulade.

⊰MO'S OPTION⊱

Blacking spice, found at any supermarket, makes crab cakes spicier;
add a little if that's the way you like them.

MoNique

Vette's Apple Pie

4 Granny Smith apples, peeled, cored, and sliced

4 Gala apples, peeled, cored, and sliced

1½ cups granulated sugar

¼ cup light brown sugar

½ stick butter (or the whole stick if you really want it rich)

3 teaspoons cinnamon

DOUGH

4 cups all-purpose flour, plus more for sprinkling

4 teaspoons baking powder

½ teaspoon salt

1 cup solid vegetable shortening

1 cup buttermilk

Preheat the oven to 350 degrees.

Place the sliced apples in a sauté pan over medium heat. Add 1 cup of the granulated sugar, brown sugar, butter, 2 teaspoons of the cinnamon, and 1/3 cup of water. Cook down for about 10 minutes, until you get a sauce but not so long that the apples get soft. Set aside.

To make the dough, thoroughly mix the flour, baking powder, and salt with a large fork. Cut in the shortening until the mixture is crumbly. Stir in the buttermilk, just until the liquid pulls the dry ingredients together into a loose ball. Divide the dough in half. Refrigerate for 30 minutes. Sprinkle some flour on a flat surface. Roll out half the dough, then cut into quarter-size rounds. Fold the rounds in half and place on a cookie sheet. Bake until brown. Set aside.

Butter an oblong baking dish. Take half of the remaining dough and roll it out to fit the bottom of the dish. Pour the apple mixture onto the dough. Work pieces of the baked dough into the fruit and sprinkle the other teaspoon of cinnamon into the mixture. Roll out the remaining dough and cut into ½-inch- to 1-inch-wide strips. Arrange the strips into a lattice pattern (crisscrossed like a basket) across the apples. Sprinkle the remaining granulated sugar lightly over the crust. Bake for 30 minutes, until the crust is golden brown and flaky.

⊁⊹ MO'S BEVERAGE ⊹⊱

Long Island Iced Tea: Mix 1 part vodka, 1 part tequila, 1 part rum, 1 part gin, 1 part triple sec, 1½ parts sweet-and-sour mix, and a splash of Coca-Cola. Combine the ingredients with ice in a glass. Pour into a shaker and give one brisk shake. Pour back into the glass and make sure there is a touch of fizz at the top. Garnish with lemon.

Mo'Nique

THE MOOD *Setting* WITH FOOD

When it comes to spicing up one's love life, dinner and a movie's cool, though a bit run-of-the-mill. A weekend away is always nice, but not very imaginative. And getting or giving a massage is a generous gesture, but it's over before you know it. Besides, there isn't always a lot of time for drawn out romantic gestures with crazy work schedules, kids, and responsibilities. Sometimes money is so funny that a weekend away is out of the question. You've got to make the most of where you are and what you've got. What's needed in a situation like this? Cleverness—and this anecdote definitely takes the cake.

A cousin, Beverly, wanted to put the spark back into her marriage, so she decided to get creative and surprise her husband with a special treat when he arrived home from the office. She went into the kitchen, got one of the big, silver serving dishes out of the cupboard, and placed it in the center of the dining room table. Then she gathered some bananas, strawberries, grapes, a can of whipped cream, an assortment of nuts, and chocolate syrup, and arranged them around the platter. When she heard her husband's car pull into the driveway, girlfriend climbed on the table and struck her sexiest pose. Baby, when he opened the door, he found his naked wife, strategically placed in the middle of the platter with a big, inviting smile. Talk about surprised—and happy. Baby, that man could hardly contain himself. In no time flat, he dropped his briefcase—and his drawers—and they got busy right there. So busy they damn near broke the table. Afterward, they didn't have to go far for food because there was plenty right there to enjoy.

I love it. Now, that's how you set a mood. See, Beverly's my kind of girl. Any woman who can skillfully incorporate food into romance is a woman after my own heart. Like I've said, ladies, the key to setting a romantic mood is out-of-the-box thinking. Beverly's husband was so happy, the next weekend, he hooked her up with a little something special, too—diamonds.

Inspired by Beverly, this menu is perfect when friends drop by (or just one special friend) and there isn't much in the fridge, but you still want to make an impression. The beauty of this one is that there's no cooking involved—but presentation is key.

Now, go get busy!

Mo'Nique

Salami
Figs
Water crackers
Brie
Cheddar
Strawberries
Grapes
Olives
Serves 2 to 4

⇥ MO'S TIP ⇤

Figs are purportedly an aphrodisiac. Chocolate and oysters, too. Soul singer Jill Scott's songs "Whatever" and "Exclusively" are perfect grooves to set a romantic mood.

⇥ MO'S BEVERAGE ⇤

Don't forget the best aphrodisiac of all—champagne! Moët, perhaps, or a bottle of Cristal for big spenders, helps to set the mood. If you're on a budget, try a sparkling wine from California. For a pretty presentation, drop a strawberry or two in each glass, or somewhere else for an amorous advance.

First DINNER

Cooking for someone special can be a scary proposition, especially if you've been good friends your entire life and suddenly become lovers. That's what happened with my husband Sid and me. When we met at Randallstown High School, neither of us imagined we'd be married, with children, especially as he was the shoulder I often cried on whenever I was going through boyfriend blues. He knew me when my desire to be famous was just a dream.

Our dream romance began after I met with the director of *Domino*, which was my first blockbuster film. After the meeting I arrived at Sid's apartment wearing a red dress. He handed me a glass of German wine (that's Sid) and offered an appetizer of sushi crab rolls that we nibbled on until dinner was ready. Simmering on the stove was his famous Tiger Chicken and Shrimp with peppers. It smelled wonderful.

Now, Sid has always been a very laid-back man. Nothing seems to ruffle his feathers, but there was no denying that the poem he had written for me—which went from cute to vulgar in a matter of seconds—put it all on the line and could only be appreciated after a few glasses of his German wine. I was so touched. But what really sealed the deal was dinner. It was perfect. He knows I like my food spicy and that's exactly how his Tiger Chicken and Shrimp was—hot!

He tells people this dish can bring out the tiger in anyone. Guess he's right because things really jumped off after that—so much so, that we eventually had a disco-themed wedding!

Tiger Chicken and Shrimp with Peppers, Onions, and Mushrooms

Tiger Chicken and Shrimp with Peppers, Onions, and Mushrooms
Rice
Broccoli with Olive Oil and Garlic
Serves 2

2 tablespoons olive oil

6 ounces boneless chicken breast, cubed

1 pint white button mushrooms, halved

1 small white onion, chopped

1 red bell pepper, seeded and chopped

1 green bell pepper, seeded and chopped

8 medium shrimp, peeled and deveined

Salt and freshly ground black pepper

1 bottle Luzianne Tiger sauce or other sweet-and-sour sauce

Heat the oil in a sauté pan on high flame. Add the chicken and sear on all sides. Follow with the mushrooms, onion, peppers, and shrimp. Season with salt and pepper and sauté briefly. Pour in the Luzianne Tiger sauce and let the dish simmer for 8 to 12 minutes.

Mo'Nique

Broccoli with Olive Oil and Garlic

Kosher salt

2 heads broccoli

2 tablespoons olive oil

3/4 cup (1 ½ sticks) unsalted butter

1 tablespoon minced garlic

Garlic salt

Freshly ground white pepper

Bring 4 quarts of water to a boil. Add a pinch of salt. Cut off the stems of the broccoli. Cut the heads into bite-size pieces and rinse well. Put the broccoli in the pot and boil gently for 6 to 8 minutes, until tender but still bright green. Drain. Set the pot back over low heat and add the olive oil, butter, and garlic. Sauté briefly until the garlic releases its fragrance. Add the broccoli. Season with the salts and the pepper, cover, and simmer over low heat for about 2 minutes. Serve.

⇥ MO'S BEVERAGE ⇤

If you enjoy wine, try a fine, dry chilled Riesling with this menu.

Summertime
AND THE LIVIN' IS EASY

You learn a lot about family at summertime backyard barbecues. Something about warm weather, good food, and endless drinking causes folks to lose their damn minds. And it never fails: someone shows up and embarrasses themselves and all you can do is laugh and shake your head and wonder how you got into this group of folks. Well, my family is no exception. We've got a few characters that always make summertime memorable.

I've got a cousin named David, who cannot hold his liquor—at all. Baby, one drop of Jack Daniel's is like truth serum to this man. And once he gets a sip, all the family gossip is revealed. David will tell you who's dating whom, who's sleeping with whom. Who's about to get a divorce. Who's about to lose their house. Who's cheatin' on their husband or wife. And who the hell is broke. Every year, David would get escorted out of the barbecue because he didn't know how to keep his mouth shut. I've also got an uncle (who shall remain nameless) that would get so torn up he'd pee down the banister because he couldn't make it to the bathroom in time, and an aunt who, even at age sixty-three, still loves to cuss and fight. And it isn't just family members that are funny. Over the years, there've been some crazy friends who've dropped by and have been a trip, too. One year a friend of the family showed up with a dozen corn muffins. Who the hell eats corn muffins at a barbecue? I guess he didn't want to arrive empty-handed and that's all he could afford to bring. That one still gets a laugh after all these years.

Despite the lunacy, I love my people and the memories we've created over the years. Ours may not be a perfect family, but that's what makes them special. I wouldn't trade them or their craziness for the world!

Sirloin Cheeseburgers
Baked Beans
Seafood Salad
Potato Salad
Strawberry Margaritas
Serves 4 to 6

Sirloin Cheeseburgers

3 pounds ground beef

2 teaspoons minced garlic

2 tablespoons chopped shallots

2 teaspoons fresh flat-leaf parsley

2 large eggs

3 tablespoons Worcestershire sauce

1 teaspoon cayenne

2 teaspoons salt

1 teaspoon freshly ground black pepper, plus more for sprinkling

1 tablespoon bread crumbs

6 sourdough hamburger buns

Mayonnaise

Dijon mustard

1 large tomato, sliced

12 slices Cheddar cheese

In a large glass bowl, combine the ground beef, garlic, shallots, parsley, eggs, Worcestershire, cayenne, salt, and pepper, and mix well. Add the bread crumbs and combine.

Divide the mixture into 6 patties. Heat and oil the grill (or a grill pan if you're doing it on the stove). When the grill is nice and hot, start to cook the burgers. For rare burgers, cook 3 to 4 minutes on each side; for well-done, make it 6 to 9 minutes on each side.

112

Lightly toast the hamburger buns on the grill, then spread each bottom half with 1 tablespoon mayonnaise and 1 teaspoon Dijon mustard. Place a slice of tomato on each bottom and sprinkle with pepper. Remove the burgers from the grill and let them rest for a minute on paper towels to absorb excess oil. Place the burgers on the bottoms, top with 2 slices of cheese and the bun tops, and serve.

⊣MO'S OPTIONS⊢

Top the burgers with a few slices of bacon, or for a different flavor,
try goat cheese or blue cheese instead of Cheddar.

⊣MO'S TIP⊢

There's one song we play at every family gathering, and that's the classic
"Family Reunion" by the O'Jays. Check it out at your next get-together.

Baked Beans

3 tablespoons vegetable oil

½ cup chopped white onion

¼ pound ground turkey

2 (28-ounce) cans baked beans

1 cup Kraft barbecue sauce

¼ cup light brown sugar

2 tablespoons granulated sugar

¼ cup Aunt Jemima's syrup

1 tablespoon mustard

2 tablespoons ground cinnamon

¼ cup grated Cheddar cheese

Preheat the oven to 350 degrees.

Heat the oil in a medium saucepot over high flame. Sauté the onion and ground turkey for 4 to 6 minutes. Add the baked beans and all of the remaining ingredients except the cheese. Mix well and bring to a simmer. Pour into a baking dish, sprinkle with the cheese, and bake for 10 to 15 minutes, until bubbly.

⇥MO'S OPTION⇤

Bush's original baked beans seasoned with bacon and brown sugar are great without much doctoring, especially if you don't have all the ingredients for this recipe on hand.

Mo'Nique

Seafood Salad

Salt

2 pounds elbow macaroni

½ cup diced celery

½ cup diced onion

½ cup diced green onions

½ pound cooked shrimp, peeled, deveined, and chopped

½ pound lump crabmeat, picked over for shells and cartilage

3 tablespoons mayonnaise

Pinch of dried parsley

1 teaspoon seasoning salt (I like McCormick's Season-All)

2 teaspoons Old Bay seasoning

Freshly ground black pepper

Bring a large pot of water to a boil and add some salt. Cook the pasta for 8 to 10 minutes, until done to your liking. Drain the pasta and run it under cold water, making sure the pasta has cooled. In a large bowl, combine the pasta with the remaining ingredients. Season with salt and pepper and serve.

⇥MO'S OPTION⇤

Use imitation crabmeat instead of real for this one. Real is fine but imitation lasts longer.

Potato Salad

5 medium Idaho potatoes

1 small white onion, thinly sliced

3 celery stalks, diced

4 hard-boiled eggs, diced

1 tablespoon sweet relish

1 cup mayonnaise

2 tablespoons Dijon mustard

1 teaspoon cayenne

Salt and freshly ground black pepper

Peel the potatoes and cover them with cold water until ready to use. Once all of the potatoes are peeled, cut them into medium cubes, and place them in a large pot with cold water to cover. Bring the water to a boil, reduce to a simmer, and cook for 15 to 20 minutes, until easily pierced with a knife. Drain the potatoes and cool. In a large bowl, combine the potatoes with the remaining ingredients. Season with salt and pepper. Refrigerate until ready to serve.

⊰MO'S BEVERAGE⊱

Backyard barbecues aren't complete without your favorite beer and
a never-ending batch of margaritas!

Mo'Nique

Strawberry Margaritas

8 cups crushed ice

8 ounces frozen whole strawberries

6 ounces tequila

4 ounces frozen limeade concentrate

2 ounces triple sec

Throw everything in a blender and blend until smooth. Blend this in two batches if necessary. Serve in chilled glasses.

Comfort
FOOD MENUS NOS. 1 & 2

What exactly is comfort food, anyway? You hear the name thrown around a lot. To me, it's meat loaf with mashed potatoes prepared so damn light and fluffy it makes everything feel okay in the midst of a storm—whether outside or during a personal one. It's the sort of food that tastes good going down, and you just can't get enough of it. Whether it's beef stew slow simmered with onions and potatoes in a rich brown gravy that you can scoop up with a big spoon or sop up with a piece of bread, a Crock-Pot of chicken with tomatoes and onions, or a simple grilled cheese sandwich accompanied by a hearty bowl of soup, comfort foods have folks fussin' and cussin' because they missed out on the last piece of fried fish.

Growing up, my grandmother Mimmie's kitchen offered some of my favorite comfort foods, especially when she made her shepherd's pie. Baby, that layer of whipped mashed potatoes seemed to float in my mouth like a billowy cloud whenever I was lucky enough to get it. Mimmie used to say that it was her way of getting us to eat our vegetables. What she didn't know is that she didn't have to bribe me because her culinary creations were simply to die for. I could never get enough.

Over the years, I've perfected my grandmother's recipe. Whenever I make it for dinner, it's a definite crowd-pleaser. Here are two menus to prepare and share, featuring my favorite comfort foods.

Shepherd's Pie

8 large Idaho potatoes

About 1 cup light cream

1 cup (2 sticks) salted butter

1 tablespoon canola oil

1 large white onion, diced

2 pounds lean ground beef or ground turkey

Seasoning salt

Freshly ground black pepper

3 (8-ounce) bags frozen mixed vegetables, thawed

1 (14-ounce) can corn, drained

**Shepherd's Pie
Stewed Tomatoes
Serves 4**

119

Preheat the oven to 325 degrees.

Peel the potatoes and cover with cold water until they are all peeled. Cut the potatoes into medium dice and place them in a large pot with cold water to cover. Bring to a boil, reduce the heat slightly, and simmer for 15 to 20 minutes, until the potatoes are tender. Drain and mash the potatoes. Add the cream and butter, a few tablespoons at a time, stirring vigorously, to get a smooth, fluffy consistency.

In a large sauté pan, heat the oil over a high flame and sauté the onion briefly. Crumble in the ground beef. Season with a little seasoning salt and pepper, and brown the beef. Add the mixed vegetables and the corn and cook over medium-high heat for 3 to 5 minutes. Scrape the beef mixture into a large pie tin or baking dish and spread over the bottom. Spoon the mashed potatoes on top, covering the beef completely. Bake for 10 to 15 minutes, until the potatoes are nice and browned.

Stewed Tomatoes

8 to 10 plum tomatoes
2 small white onions, chopped
½ celery stalk, finely chopped
½ green pepper, seeded and finely chopped
1 tablespoon sugar
1 teaspoon salt, or a little less
1 tablespoon cornstarch

Fill a pot with water and bring to a boil. Cut a small X on the bottom of each tomato (opposite the stem end) and drop into the hot water. When the skin starts to peel back at the X (in about 30 seconds), remove the tomatoes and, as soon as they're cool enough to handle, slide them out of their skins. Cut into small pieces and place in a medium pot with the onions, celery, pepper, sugar, and salt. Simmer over medium heat for about 10 minutes. Mix the cornstarch with ½ cup of cold water, until smooth. Slowly stir the cornstarch into the tomatoes and simmer for about 2 minutes more.

⊱MO'S OPTION⊰

You can also doctor up S&W stewed tomatoes.
Substitute 2 (15-ounce) cans stewed tomatoes for the plum
tomatoes and proceed with the recipe.

Mo'Nique

Meat Loaf

1½ pounds lean ground beef or turkey

½ pound ground pork

1 large white onion, diced

2 celery stalks, diced

1 tablespoon chopped garlic

1 (15-ounce) can crushed plum tomatoes

1 green bell pepper, seeded and diced

2 tablespoons Worcestershire sauce

2 tablespoons Dijon mustard

1 teaspoon salt

¼ teaspoon freshly ground black pepper

1 cup bread crumbs

2 large eggs, beaten

1 cup ketchup

Juice of 1 lemon

Meat Loaf
Roasted Garlic Potatoes
Sautéed Spinach
Serves 4

Preheat the oven to 325 degrees.

In a large bowl, mix the beef, pork, onion, celery, garlic, tomatoes, green pepper, Worcestershire, mustard, salt, and pepper. Add the bread crumbs and eggs, and, with your hands, combine thoroughly. Form into a loaf shape and place in a lightly oiled loaf pan. Bake for 30 minutes.

While the meat loaf is cooking, whisk together the ketchup, lemon juice, and 1 tablespoon water and some salt and pepper. After the meat loaf has baked for 30 minutes, pour the ketchup mixture over the top. Return it to the oven and bake for 10 to 15 minutes more, or to your desired doneness. Let the loaf cool a bit before cutting.

Roasted Garlic Potatoes

5 Red Bee potatoes, quartered
1 tablespoon minced garlic
1 tablespoon chopped shallots
1 tablespoon chopped fresh rosemary
1 tablespoon chopped fresh thyme
2 tablespoons butter

Preheat the oven to 325 degrees.

In a bowl, mix the potatoes, garlic, shallots, rosemary, and thyme. Spread on a greased baking dish and top with pieces of the butter. Roast the potatoes in the oven for 20 to 30 minutes, until the potatoes are tender when pierced with a knife.

Mo'Nique

Sautéed Spinach

2 tablespoons olive oil

1 tablespoon unsalted butter

1 tablespoon minced garlic

2 shallots, diced

2 pounds spinach, cleaned

1 teaspoon kosher salt

1 teaspoon freshly ground black pepper

In a medium sauté pan heat the oil and butter over a medium flame. Add the garlic and shallots, and sauté for 10 seconds before adding the spinach and the salt and pepper. Sauté for about 3 minutes, stirring constantly. Don't overcook; the spinach should be a nice green color.

Comfort
FOOD MENU NO. 3

Over the years, pork has gotten a bad rap. I don't know why, because the "other" white meat is some of the most tender and tasty meat you can eat. Now, I'm not saying that pork should be a daily staple of one's diet. Too much of a good thing too often can be detrimental to anyone's health—but every now and then, if prepared just right, swine can be divine! Barbecued baby back ribs, spareribs, crispy bacon, and pig's feet are among my favorites.

Back in the day, before first-class flights were a part of my contract, I flew the friendly skies in coach. And that was in the days when airlines fed you. Though it wasn't a lot, you could pretty much count on a morsel or two of chicken, a sad little salad, and a brownie wrapped in plastic to make the flight a bit more comfortable. Well, not today! Baby, you better show up with your own grub because the airlines aren't passing out anything but peanuts and pretzels these days. And who can get comfortable with that?—especially after a grueling workday, or a six-hour flight from New York to Los Angeles.

During the first season as the host of *It's Showtime at the Apollo*, I had to rush directly from the show to John F. Kennedy Airport to make a flight home. Baby, I was so hungry, I had a headache. It was an afternoon flight, and I was anticipating that airplane meal. But that's not what I got. When the flight attendant came around, she offered me a choice of a yogurt bar, a bagel, or a banana. Now, I didn't want any of that mess. What I wanted was what they were serving in first class—warm nuts, nonstop drinks, a nice tossed salad, filet mignon, warm rolls with butter, and the chocolate chip cookies that the entire coach cabin could smell as they were baking. I went from hungry to angry because they ought not to tease folks in coach with freshly baked cookies—and we can't have any. That's downright rude.

But the flight attendant turned out to be a cool sistah who obviously felt my pain because during the dinner hour, she walked by and placed a napkin on my tray. Wrapped up in it was one of those freshly baked, warm first-class cookies. I went from pissed to quite pleased and savored that little cookie like it was a steak.

See, that's the power of food—it comforts, even on a six-hour flight. But I was still hungry when we landed, so you know when I walked into my house and smelled the wonderful aroma of spareribs, the last thing on my mind was whether or not it was pork. All I wanted to know was, Does it taste as good as it smells?, and if so, please fix me a plate. When I bit into those succulent spareribs, that long plane ride was a distant memory. That's what a good meal will do. Cure a headache. Help you put up with people who work your nerves. And give you an overall attitude adjustment.

This menu features another of my favorites—fried pork chops with rice and gravy. After trying this one, check out just how comfortable (and sleepy) you'll feel, too.

Mo'Nique

Fried Pork Chops

4 (8-ounce) pork chops

1 teaspoon chopped fresh thyme

1 teaspoon chopped fresh rosemary

1 teaspoon kosher salt

2 teaspoons garlic salt

2 teaspoons seasoning salt

1 cup canola oil

2 cups all-purpose flour

2 tablespoons unsalted butter

2 celery stalks, diced

2 white onions, diced

3 garlic cloves, crushed

3 cups chicken stock

127

Wash the pork chops and pat them dry. Combine the fresh herbs and salts and season the chops on both sides. Heat the oil in a cast-iron skillet over a high flame. Dredge the chops in about ½ cup of the flour and shake off any excess. Lay the chops into the skillet and cook for 7 to 8 minutes on each side until nicely browned and crispy. Remove the chops to a plate and set aside.

Carefully drain the oil from the pan, leaving about ¼ cup. Gradually whisk the remaining flour into the oil in the skillet and adjust the heat to a medium simmer. Cook the roux until it begins to darken. Add the butter, celery, onion, garlic, and the stock. Stir until it thickens and starts to simmer. Put the chops back into the pan, cover, and cook for another 15 to 20 minutes.

Dirty Rice

1½ cups white long-grain rice

1 tablespoon olive oil

½ small white onion, diced

1 teaspoon minced garlic

½ red bell pepper, diced

1 jalapeño, seeded and diced

1 cup Brown Gravy (recipe follows)

1 tablespoon unsalted butter

Salt and freshly ground black pepper

Wash the rice in a strainer. In a medium saucepan, heat the olive oil and sauté the onion, garlic, and peppers for 1 minute. Add the rice and 3⅓ cups cold water. Bring to a boil, then reduce the heat to low, cover, and simmer for 15 minutes. Stir in the brown gravy and the butter, and season with salt and pepper. Cover and simmer for 6 to 8 minutes more. Mix well and serve.

⊱MO'S OPTION⊰

Zatarain's dirty rice with cheese is a great substitute
if you don't have time to make this rice dish from scratch.

Mo'Nique

Brown Gravy

1 tablespoon olive oil

2 small white onions, diced

5 tablespoons unsalted butter

3 tablespoons all-purpose flour

2 cups chicken stock or water

1 teaspoon chopped fresh rosemary

1 teaspoon chopped fresh thyme

2 garlic cloves, chopped (1 teaspoon)

Salt

Freshly ground black pepper

Heat the olive oil in a saucepan over a high flame and sauté the onions, reducing the heat to medium, for 10 to 15 minutes (or 7 to 10 minutes for a lighter gravy). Add the butter, and once it is melted, whisk in the flour. Cook, stirring, for 3 to 5 minutes until the flour is nice and brown. Add the stock, herbs, and garlic, and simmer over medium heat until the gravy thickens. Season with salt and pepper. This recipe will make about 3 cups of gravy.

Comfort
FOOD MENU NO. 4

Pregnancy the second time around was a trip! For one, I was sixteen years older than the first time. And though I should've taken it easy, as the doctor recommended, I've never been one to sit around the house all day, nesting, and doing nothing. I've got to be out among the people, doing things, and working. That's what I did until one of my babies shut that down.

Despite my delicate condition, I taped my Oxygen network television special, *Mo'Nique's F.A.T. Chance*, while four months pregnant, and was ready to hop on an airplane to New York to shoot fifteen episodes of my other gig as host of *It's Showtime at the Apollo*. That is, until my doctor said, "No, ma'am. You must shut it down. No traveling for you." So I did—for a few weeks. But soon, I was back at it again, decorating the nursery, having lunch with friends, and climbing the stairs. I ripped and ran so much that, eventually, I ran myself into early labor pains that sent me to the hospital, where I remained until my delivery. Oh, did I mention this happened four days before a big baby shower that friends had planned for me? That's right! I told them, "Don't stop the party. Go on without me." They did. And they taped it for me, so I could see what I missed.

Good food is one of the things I missed most while in the hospital. Though I didn't experience any real cravings, I did long for a few of my favorites, like chicken and dumplings. This dish soothes my soul and fills me up whenever I make it!

Chicken and Dumplings

Serves 4

3 pounds boneless, skinless chicken breasts

2 tablespoons olive or vegetable oil

Kosher salt

Seasoning salt

1 large white onion, chopped

DUMPLINGS

2½ cups all-purpose flour

4 teaspoons baking powder

Garlic salt

2 tablespoons bacon fat, melted

1 cup buttermilk

½ cup heavy cream

3 tablespoons all-purpose flour

½ cup whole milk

Wash the chicken under cold water and pat dry. Place a large stockpot over a medium flame and add the oil. Lightly season the chicken with the kosher and seasoning salts and brown well on both sides. Add the onion to the pot and cook briefly. Add enough cold water to cover the chicken. Bring to a boil, reduce to a low simmer, and cover the pot. Cook for 25 minutes. If the broth gets too low, add a little water.

To make the dumplings, mix the flour, baking powder, and a pinch of garlic salt in a bowl. Slowly add the bacon fat, stirring well to integrate. Stir in the buttermilk until a dough forms. Set aside.

In a small bowl, whisk together the cream, flour, and milk. After the chicken has cooked for 25 minutes, add the mixture to the chicken. Season the pot with garlic salt. Drop spoonfuls of the dumpling dough into the pot with the chicken. Cook for 10 to 15 minutes on low heat and serve.

Steak
STEVE IMES

My brother Steve is quite a character. After a brief career as a computer programmer with the FBI, he decided to try his hand at comedy. That in itself was a joke because he bombed so bad at an open mic night that they turned the mic off in the middle of his performance. I teased him so much he dared me to get onstage and try it, so I did and got a standing ovation. I had found my calling and it was comedy. Steve found his, too. He became my manager and negotiated my first deal, hosting a hair show for twenty-five dollars. Since then, we've built quite a career—sold-out arenas, three hit television shows, several feature films, and more—and have gone from franks and beans to steak and lobster.

Like a lot of men, Steve has a signature dish he does well. So well, he calls it his Steak Steve Imes: a grilled porterhouse steak with peppers and onions and a side of buttered noodles. Whenever he makes it, the entire process turns into a ritual. First, he marinates the steaks, and then he goes to work, meticulously chopping up all the peppers and onions. Mind you, all of this is going on while he's sipping a drink (I don't know what it is about cooking and drinking in my family but it goes hand in hand) and playing his favorite house music. He also throws on his favorite manly apron (it says "Kiss the Cook") and gets his dance on as he fires up the grill. I must admit, the result is a damn good steak. Anytime he makes it, we still fight for the fat piece of meat.

I present to you Steak Steve Imes.

Porterhouse Steaks

Porterhouse Steaks
Buttered Noodles
Serves 4

4 (16-ounce) porterhouse steaks

¼ cup olive oil, plus more for rubbing

3 tablespoons seasoning salt

3 tablespoons coarse salt

3 tablespoons garlic salt

3 tablespoons cracked black peppercorns

1 tablespoon minced garlic

10 sprigs fresh rosemary, stemmed and chopped

6 white onions, coarsely chopped

5 bell peppers, coarsely chopped

134

Prepare the grill or preheat the oven to 350 degrees.

Rub the steaks with olive oil and season them with the salts, peppercorns, garlic, and rosemary. Heat about ¼ cup of the olive oil in a large sauté pan over a medium flame and sauté the onions and peppers.

Place the steaks on the hot grill and cook, turning several times until the desired doneness is reached. Indoors, sear the steaks on both sides in a sauté pan, then transfer them to the oven for 15 to 20 minutes for a perfect medium steak.

Top the steaks with sautéed onions and peppers and serve over buttered egg noodles.

Buttered Noodles

1 pound pasta (Steve does egg noodles)

1 stick unsalted butter

½ cup chopped flat-leaf parsley

3 tablespoons olive oil

Salt and freshly ground black pepper

Bring a large pot of salted water to a boil. Add the pasta and stir with a large fork. Return the water to a gentle boil and cook for 8 to 10 minutes. Drain the pasta and transfer it to a serving bowl. Add the butter, parsley, olive oil, and salt and pepper. Toss well and serve.

135

The
BIG GIRL'S WORKOUT SALAD

Let me dispel a myth about Big Girls right here. Contrary to popular belief, we do eat more than oxtails, pig's feet, and fried chicken, and we do work out. I just don't kill myself doin' it. In fact, after *The Parkers* ended, I decided to focus on my health. Every year, the studio requires that we take a physical. And though I'm a Big Girl, I'm also a healthy one. But like everyone, my goal is to combat the things that happen as we age—a slower metabolism, aches and pains, the struggle for overall good health and well-being. So, I started walking with a girlfriend on the beach. A funny thing happened: it changed my life. Folks started to see a shapelier Mo.

The thing that's cool about this workout is that we didn't kill ourselves. It was just one foot in front of the other at our own pace, and before we knew it, one mile had turned into two, two into three, and soon, we were up to ten. During those times we'd reflect, renew, refocus, and even cry, laugh, or complain about whatever life threw at us. More than the company, I enjoyed getting out in the fresh air and taking control of my health. In no time, my pants got looser (I lost inches, not weight), I felt better, and people began to notice.

To this day, I still get my workout on. Sometimes it's still a walk on the beach, or a climb up the Santa Monica stairs (which can be brutal because there are at least eighty of them). And afterward, I'm usually hungry. If I'm in the mood for fried chicken, then I'll have some—on a salad. I don't believe folks should deprive themselves of the things they love. You just can't eat as much of them.

Some might call this one a cobb salad, but where I come from, it's called a lunchmeat salad, and it's filled with plenty of protein.

Lunchmeat Salad

1 head butter lettuce

1 romaine heart

½ head iceberg lettuce

2 plum tomatoes

1 avocado

4 ounces crumbled blue cheese (1 cup)

1 ounce grated mozzarella cheese

3 to 4 crisp cooked bacon slices

2 hard-boiled eggs, peeled and chopped

2 to 4 ounces turkey, chopped or sliced

2 to 4 ounces ham

1 ounce salami (optional)

2 (8-ounce) boneless, skinless chicken breasts, sliced (precooked from deli)

1 can corn kernels (or fresh, cut off the cob)

Lunchmeat Salad
Mustard and Garlic Dressing
Mint iced tea
Serves 1

137

Wash the lettuces and chop into bite-size pieces. Put in a large bowl and toss. Chop the tomato. Peel and chop the avocado. Sprinkle these and all other ingredients into the bowl. Mix well and serve with Mustard and Garlic Dressing (recipe follows).

┤► MO'S TIP ►

Serve the salad with a piece of warm garlic toast.

Mustard and Garlic Dressing

1 shallot, chopped

1 garlic clove, minced

1 (9-ounce) jar capers, and 4 tablespoons caper juice

1 tablespoon freshly ground black pepper

2 tablespoons Worcestershire sauce

3 egg yolks

6 tablespoons Dijon mustard

½ cup olive oil

1 cup canola oil

½ cup lemon juice

2 cups red wine vinegar

Combine the shallots, garlic, capers, caper juice, pepper, and Worcestershire in a blender. Pulse to a fine paste. Set aside.

In a medium bowl, combine the egg yolks and mustard, whisking together until smooth. Slowly stir in the olive oil and canola oil until completely mixed, then add half of the paste, checking the seasoning. Add more or less of the paste, based on your desired flavor, followed by the lemon juice and vinegar. Whisk thoroughly. This recipe makes about 2 cups of dressing. Leftovers will keep in the refrigerator for a week.

Mo'Nique

Sunday SUPPER

Ever wonder what happened to family dinner hour? Well, the tradition is still alive in my mother's house. My earliest recollection of eating great meals started in my mother's kitchen at dinnertime. Despite working long hours as a quality control manager at Westinghouse, with a husband and four kids (Steve, Millicent, me, and our older brother, Gerald) to feed, Miss Alice always found a way to have dinner on the table promptly at six o'clock and we'd sit down and enjoy it together. Not much has changed since then. Even though it's just her and my father now, dinnertime at her house is still six, and though she enjoys it whenever one of us stops by for dinner, we know that by seven o'clock Miss Alice's kitchen is scrubbed clean and closed—and when the kitchen's closed, it stays closed.

Growing up, Steve didn't seem to get that message because he'd stroll in late, regularly, with the same question, "What's for dinner?" My mother would tell him we had steak, baked potatoes, and string beans—which were all favorites of his. Even if he wanted one, he wasn't getting a plate. It was either PB&J (that's peanut butter and jelly) or go to bed hungry. This was in the days before microwaves, when leftovers meant messing up the kitchen again. That was bad news for Steve but wonderful for the rest of us because those extra helpings always hit the spot. Eventually, Steve figured out how to come in late—and still get a plate. He may not have started with us, but he made sure he got there on time to finish.

Next weekend, try this Sunday Supper and tell everyone that dinner will be served promptly at six o'clock—and they better not be late because after that, the kitchen's closed.

Smothered Chicken

2 cups canola oil

1 (3-pound) chicken, cut into pieces

1 teaspoon salt

2 teaspoons garlic salt

2 teaspoons seasoning salt

1 teaspoon chopped fresh thyme

1 teaspoon chopped fresh rosemary

2 cups all-purpose flour

2 tablespoons unsalted butter

2 celery stalks, diced

2 small white onions, diced

3 garlic cloves, crushed

3 cups chicken stock

Smothered Chicken
Brown Gravy
Rice
Serves 4

140

Heat the oil in a large cast-iron skillet over medium-high heat. Wash the chicken, pat dry, and season well with the salts and herbs. Dredge the chicken in ½ cup of the flour and shake off any excess. Lay the chicken pieces into the hot oil and cook for 7 to 8 minutes on each side. Remove to paper towels to absorb the excess oil.

Gradually whisk the remaining 1½ cups flour into the oil remaining in the skillet, and cook over medium heat until it begins to brown. Add the butter, celery, onion, garlic, and stock and mix thoroughly. Put the chicken back into the skillet, cover, and cook for another 15 to 20 minutes.

⊰ MO'S OPTIONS ⊱

Add a few sautéed mushrooms and some
sautéed green bell peppers to the chicken.

Mo'Nique

Brown Gravy

1 tablespoon olive oil

2 small Spanish onions, sliced or diced

5 tablespoons unsalted butter

3 to 5 tablespoons all-purpose flour

1 teaspoon chopped fresh rosemary

1 teaspoon chopped fresh thyme

1 teaspoon chopped garlic

2 cups chicken stock or water

Salt

Freshly ground black pepper

Heat the olive oil over medium flame and sauté the onions for 10 to 15 minutes, until well browned. For lighter gravy, cook for about 8 minutes. Add the butter. Once the butter is melted, whisk in the flour and cook for 3 to 5 minutes until toasted to a nice deep brown. Add the herbs and garlic. Slowly whisk in the stock and simmer over medium heat until the gravy thickens. Season with salt and pepper. Serve over cooked rice.

BEET IT

Here's a lighter salad that features one of the sweetest vegetables available—beets. Some people may not be fans of the oblong root vegetable with the deep red and golden yellow flesh, but beets are loaded with potassium, folate (great if you're trying to conceive), and fiber. If you're a beet eater, enjoy this colorful and refreshing recipe. If not, give beets a chance!

Beet Salad

Serves 1 or 2

6 small beets

6 tablespoons canola oil

1 head endive, washed, and dried

3 cups arugula, trimmed, washed, and dried

6 ounces crumbled goat cheese (1½ cups)

1 red onion, thinly sliced

Scant ½ cup toasted walnuts

1 mandarin orange

BALSAMIC VINAIGRETTE

2 tablespoons Dijon mustard

2 tablespoons light brown sugar

¼ cup balsamic vinegar

2 garlic cloves, minced (1 teaspoon)

1 small shallot, minced (1 teaspoon)

5 tablespoons olive oil

Salt

Freshly ground black pepper

Preheat the oven to 350 degrees. For the beets, wash them well, pat dry, and rub with the oil. Place the beets in a baking pan, cover with aluminum foil, and roast for about 45 minutes. Remove from the oven, and, when they are cool enough to handle, peel the beets. Cool them in the refrigerator while assembling the vinaigrette.

To make the vinaigrette, simply whisk together the mustard, sugar, vinegar, garlic, shallots, and olive oil. Season with salt and pepper. Finish assembling the salad.

Mo'Nique

Combine the endive and the arugula in a large bowl. Add the goat cheese, onion, and walnuts. Peel the orange and separate it into sections; add to the bowl. Slice the beets and add. Toss everything together, drizzle with the balsamic vinaigrette, and serve.

⊱≕MO'S BEVERAGE≕⊰

I love to mix lemonade and mint iced tea, for a refreshing twist. Just mix equal parts sweetened mint iced tea and lemonade. Garnish with mint sprigs.

Souper SUPPER

Every once in a while, steak, a big fat baked potato (with sour cream, butter, and chives), and a tossed salad hits the hungry spot, especially as, unlike back in the day, it's not a problem to get it anymore. I just go to the store—or to a restaurant—and get it. But there were days when Oodles of Noodles, or a bowl of Campbell's chicken noodle soup, was dinner. There are times when I like to go back to the good old days, especially after I've been running behind two little boys who constantly keep me on the go. Souper Supper is for those times when you want something filling but don't feel like slaving in the kitchen all night.

Homemade soup is always nice, especially if it's a bowl (or two) of chicken noodle or tomato, paired with a grilled cheese sandwich. Or, if I'm feeling like something special, I love my mother's oyster stew, which is easy and quick to make, and always hits the hungry spot.

Homemade Chicken Noodle Soup

3 pounds boneless, skinless chicken breasts, cubed

1 teaspoon salt

2 tablespoons freshly ground black pepper

2 teaspoons garlic salt

1 teaspoon seasoning salt

2 tablespoons olive oil

2 tablespoons unsalted butter

3 large carrots, roughly chopped

6 celery stalks, roughly chopped

1 jumbo white onion, roughly chopped

2 garlic cloves, crushed (1 teaspoon)

4 rosemary sprigs

4 thyme sprigs

1 pound egg noodles (penne or rotelle are also nice)

Homemade Chicken Noodle Soup
Roasted Tomato Soup with Croutons
Oyster Stew
Grilled Cheese Sandwiches
Serves 4

147

Wash the chicken under cold water and pat dry. Season with the salt, pepper, garlic salt, and seasoned salt. Heat the oil in a large pot over medium flame. Melt the butter with the olive oil and sauté the chicken until it is nicely seared on all sides. Add the carrots, celery, onion, and garlic, and sauté for 2 to 3 minutes. Adjust the seasoning, if needed.

Cover the chicken and vegetables completely with cold water and add the fresh herbs. Bring to a simmer, cover, and lower the heat (until the soup just simmers). Cook for about 25 minutes. Add the pasta and cook for 15 more minutes, until the pasta is tender. Remove the thyme and rosemary sprigs, check the seasoning, and serve.

Roasted Tomato Soup with Croutons

12 large tomatoes (about 4 pounds), stemmed and quartered
½ cup extra-virgin olive oil (divided)
¼ cup good-quality balsamic vinegar
6 large garlic cloves, peeled
Salt
Freshly ground black pepper
1 cup chopped yellow onions
2 cups lightly packed fresh basil leaves, plus a few leaves for garnish

CROUTONS
1 loaf French bread
Extra-virgin olive oil
Salt

Preheat the oven to 375 degrees.

In a large bowl, mix together the tomatoes, ¼ cup of the oil, the vinegar, and the garlic. Season with salt and pepper. Spread the tomatoes out on a nonreactive baking sheet. Roast the tomatoes in the oven until very dark in spots, 35 to 40 minutes. Remove and allow to cool a bit. While the tomatoes are cooling, prepare the croutons.

To make croutons, cut the bread crosswise into slices about 1 inch thick (you will need 8 slices). Lightly brush the slices on both sides with a little olive oil and season with salt. Place the slices on a baking sheet and toast in the oven until the croutons are golden brown and just beginning to crisp, about 6 minutes.

To assemble the soup, combine the remaining ¼ cup olive oil, the onions, and a pinch of salt in a large saucepan over medium heat. Cook until the onions are very soft, 8 to 10 minutes, stirring occasionally. Add the basil and sauté with the onions for about 1 minute.

Add the roasted tomatoes and 2 cups cold water to the saucepan. Bring the mixture to a simmer and cook for 10 minutes. Season with salt and pepper. Carefully pour the tomato mixture into a blender and make sure the lid is secured. Start the blender at a slow speed and increase gradually. (You can also use an immersion blender right in the pot.) The mixture should be very smooth. You should have about 8 cups. You can prepare the soup to this point a day ahead and refrigerate. If serving, pour the soup into a medium saucepan and bring to a slow simmer over medium heat. Place 2 croutons in the center of each shallow soup bowl. Pour the soup around the croutons. Garnish with torn basil leaves.

Oyster Stew

1 cup whole milk

¾ cup (1½ sticks) butter

4 tablespoons vegetable flakes

Pinch cayenne (or ground hot red pepper)

2 teaspoons McCormick's Season-All

2 (8-ounce) cans shucked oysters, with liquid

1 to 1½ (10¾-ounce) cans Campbell's cream of potato soup

Oyster crackers (optional)

Combine the milk, butter, vegetable flakes, cayenne, seasoning salt, and the strained liquid off the oysters in a medium saucepan. Simmer for 3 to 4 minutes. Stir in the cream of potato soup to your preferred consistency, then bring back to a simmer. (The more soup you add, the thicker it will be.) Add the oysters and cook for about 7 minutes. Serve with oyster crackers, if desired.

Mo'Nique

Grilled Cheese Sandwiches

8 slices potato bread (French, sourdough, or whole wheat work, too)

2 tablespoons butter

About ½ pound mild Cheddar, thinly sliced

Make four sandwiches using 2 slices of bread and four slices of cheese for each. Slowly melt 1 tablespoon of the butter in a medium sauté pan and place 2 sandwiches in the pan. Toast lightly, about 2 minutes on each side. Repeat with the remaining butter and sandwiches. Cut each sandwich in half and serve.

⊰MO'S OPTIONS⊱

If you're a fan of another type of cheese, such as mozzarella, Havarti, or American, by all means do it your way. Or make it a double-decker with two different cheeses. I also like to add tomato or a few slices of bacon to make an ordinary grilled cheese sandwich extraordinary.

PANTRY ESSENTIALS

You never know when you'll need a spice, a stock, or a sauce. That's why my pantry is filled with essentials. Chances are you'll use them more than you realize. Here's a list of the basics.

allspice

almond extract

aluminum foil

baking powder

baking soda

basil

beans

beef stock

brown sugar (light and dark)

chicken stock

chocolate (semisweet chips, unsweetened baking chocolate, cocoa powder)

cinnamon

cornmeal

cornstarch

Crisco cooking spray (regular and butter-flavored)

Crisco oil

Crisco solid vegetable shortening

curry powder

dill

flour (all-purpose)

garlic salt

ground ginger

honey

maple syrup

noodles/pasta

nutmeg

nuts (walnuts, pecans, and almonds)

Old Bay seasoning

oregano

paper towels

pepper

pineapple (canned)

plastic wrap

rice

salt

seasoning salt

spaghetti sauce/marinara sauce

sugar (granulated and confectioners')

vanilla extract

wax paper

wooden toothpicks

yeast (active dry)

A FEW OF MY FAVORITE PRODUCT SHORTCUTS

When time is of the essence and a shortcut is the only way to go, these are a few of my favorite products. With a little doctorin' here and there, it'll taste just like homemade.

Betty Crocker Casserole Potatoes—I especially like the roasted garlic and sour cream and chives versions.

Jiffy or **Betty Crocker cornbread mix**

Bisquick Cheese-Garlic Biscuits—Great for breakfast, lunch, or dinner.

Corned beef hash—I love corned beef hash with eggs, but it's a bit time-consuming to make from scratch. That's why this is so great.

Glory Foods products—With canned, fresh, and frozen products such as black-eyed peas, collard greens, and yams, Glory Foods taste like homemade in half the time. You can add them to fresh collards if you find yourself running short on time, or if more folks show up than you've invited.

Green Giant Harvest Fresh Green Beans

Herb-Ox Chicken (and Beef) Instant Bouillon & Seasoning

Lawry's Perfect Blend for Chicken and Beef

Luzianne Seafood Coating Mix—Great for fried fish.

PAM for the Grill—This is a great spray for the grill. It keeps food from sticking and makes cleanup a breeze.

Zatarain's New Orleans Gumbo Mix

FIXING FOOD FAUX PAS

If your gravy is too thick, add water to thin it out, but not too much. Add it in slowly until you get the consistency you desire.

If your gravy is too thin, add equal amounts of cornstarch and water to thicken. Again, you don't want to add too much, so stir in slowly and constantly, checking consistency.

Are your collards too salty? Try adding sautéed spinach to the mix to absorb some of the salt, or more greens.

Overcooked cornbread can be brought back to life by melting butter and brushing it over the top just before it's served. The moisture from the butter softens it.

INDEX

159

160

159

INDEX